S0-BWL-752

THE "ESSENCE OF CHRISTIANITY"

University of South Florida
INTERNATIONAL STUDIES IN FORMATIVE CHRISTIANITY AND JUDAISM

EDITORIAL BOARD

FOR THE UNITED STATES
Jacob Neusner, University of South Florida
James Strange, University of South Florida
William Scott Green, University of Rochester
Bruce Chilton, Bard College

FOR ISRAEL
Ithamar Gruenwald, University of Tel Aviv
Mayer Gruber, Ben Gurion University of the Negev

FOR SCANDINAVIA
Karl-Gustav Sandelin, Åbo Akademi
Heikki Räisänen, University of Helsinki
Karl-Johan Illman, Åbo Akademi

FOR ITALY
Mauro Pesce, University of Bologna
Adriana Destro, University of Bologna
Pier Cesare Bori, University of Bologna

FOR GERMANY
Gerd Lüdemann, University of Göttingen

FOR AUSTRIA
Günther Stemberger, University of Vienna

FOR NEW ZEALAND
Gregory W. Dawes, University of Otago

FOR CANADA
Herbert Basser, Queens University
Harry Fox, University of Toronto
Craig Evans, Trinity Western University

VOLUME 3
THE "ESSENCE OF CHRISTIANITY"
The Hermeneutical Question in the Protestant and Modernist Debate (1897–1904)
by
Guglielmo Forni Rosa

THE "ESSENCE OF CHRISTIANITY"
THE HERMENEUTICAL QUESTION IN THE PROTESTANT AND MODERNIST DEBATE
(1897-1904)

Guglielmo Forni Rosa

Translated from the Italian
by Marisa Luciani
and Jane Stevenson

Scholars Press
Atlanta, Georgia

WITHDRAWN

THE "ESSENCE OF CHRISTIANITY"
The Hermeneutical Question in the
Protestant and Modernist Debate (1897–1904)

by
Guglielmo Forni Rosa

Published by Scholars Press
for the University of South Florida

© 1995
University of South Florida

Library of Congress Cataloging in Publication Data
Forni, Guglielmo.
    [Essenza del cristianesimo. English]
    The essence of Christianity : the hermeneutical question in the Protestant
and modernist debate (1897–1904) / Guglielmo Forni Rosa ; translated from the
Italian by Marisa Luciani and Jane Stevenson.
          p.   cm. — (University of South Florida international studies in
formative Christianity and Judaism ; v. 3)
    Includes bibliographical references.
    ISBN 0-7885-0138-0 (alk. paper)
    1. Modernism. 2. Modernism—Catholic Church. 3. Hermeneutics—Religious
aspects—Christianity. 4. Christianity—Essence, genius, nature—History of doctrines—
19th century. 5. Christianity— Essence, genius, nature—History of doctrines—20th
century. 6. Liberalism (Religion)—Protestant churches—History—19th century.
 7. Liberalism (Religion)—Protestant churches—History—20th century. 8. Harnack,
Adolf von, 1851–1930. Wesen des Christentums. 9. Catholic Church—Doctrines—
History—20th century. I. Title. II. Series.
BT82.F6713   1995
230'.01—dc20   95-30173
                                   CIP

Printed in the United States of America
on acid-free paper

Table of Contents

Introduction

The problems that lie at the origins of this book are contemporary problems. We sought for traces of them in the documents of a relatively recent past, fully aware however that they have not really been solved even within our present cultural context; on the contrary, it could be said that they were dramatically present to the generation we are going to be dealing with, after which they led a fairly arduous life and, in certain cases or contexts, ended up completely forgotten.

First and foremost there is a problem of general or fundamental hermeneutics. It is a known fact that modernising tendencies stressed subjectivity, interiority and freedom in the interpretation of the Scriptures and of religious documents in general; in their fight against intellectualism and scholastic objectivism, Protestants and modernist Catholics rejected everything which, as Laberthonnière said, comes to us from the outside and in the face of which we are merely passive. However, in so far as we are dealing with Christianity, we are also forced to recognise that interpretation, in its Christological and trinitarian movement, is in particular faithfulness and imitation; that is to say, that a certain conscious and explicit repetition of the founding experiences cannot be without a dimension of objectivity. Even when scholastic objectivism is contested, as it is by the modernists, it must be recognised that the superiority of the message over, or its independence of, those who bear witness to it remains an absolutely decisive element in the Christian understanding of the world. The essential has already taken place: Christ, in obedience to the Father unto death, has saved humanity and given it life. The task of the Christian is to follow the same movement, to be the faithful expression of the visible form of the Saviour. The originality or independence that can be seen in the various forms of Christianity in the course of history comes from the diversity of men, cultures and ages: it is not sought intentionally by the true witness of Christ, who, on the contrary, wishes to disappear, to efface himself in the imitation of his Lord. In other words, it seems that the Christian message indicates clearly a resistence to the individualistic, sentimental pulverisation typical of "democratic" modernity, and that, after all the analyses and counter-analyses of the fall of the principle of authority, of the need for active interiorisation and for a Christian life (Blondel, Laberthonnière), this resistence should be fundamentally conserved.

Modern development has without doubt taught us that religious faithfulness cannot be reduced to abstract assent, to the observance of formulas and doctrines; but the relationship with the Father that Christ lived and taught (a relationship of pure obedience, of faithful submission) is the model for every relationship that man establishes with the divine within Christianity. This means that, notwithstanding all the work done during this century, modern hermeneutics and Christian hermeneutics could be divergent; this would not lead us to a choice which would necessarily be an impoverishment or a regression, but rather would give us a greater awareness of the diversity of cultures that are superimposed in our experience. Is it then true to state what has today become almost a commonplace: that Christianity does not need specific hermeneutics and that the general hermeneutics of today's secular culture is all we need for an understanding of the Scriptures?

A second problem from which we started our investigation is that in the theological and philosophical-religious literature the notion of "historical fact" remains largely undefined. The faithfulness we have spoken of is faithfulness to concrete events: the life, death and Resurrection of Christ; but these events are not fully acknowledged by historical science and require a different frame of reference, which for Christianity is apostolic transmission, the tradition of the Church. Now, when theology points out that the Church has its centre in events that precede it and surpass it, it is constantly tempted (maybe to accredit its affirmations for secular culture) to take these events as historical facts, in the sense of their being fully real and verifiable, also profanely speaking; at the same time it is aware that these "facts" possess various characteristics that make them extraordinary and non-worldly and that are not, and cannot be, completely acknowledged by scientific inquiry. In this respect, even if historicity (that is, the *objectivity* of an event belonging to the past) is required for the life of Christ, taken in the fullness of its theological attributes, this life is the constantly renewed result of the believing memory (which thinks of Christ both as a *historical* figure and as the *Risen Christ*) and not only of historical studies. This oscillation, this necessary yet unfinished dialogue between faith and science, permeates the notion of historical fact.

Probably — and it is here that we state our third problem — different criteria of objectivity or of reality are valid in reference to different communities, in this case the scientific community and the believing community. This gap may be narrowed if objectivity (past reality or, in another sense, the binding nature of norms) is not seen as a jealous and exclusive possession deriving from a single approach, but if the contemporary condition is understood as being characterised by a legitimate plurality of methods and of cognitive needs. As for our topic, the times of Modernism are over, the times when historical science could refuse to acknowledge the legitimacy of tradition as a source of knowledge of the past, and in its turn was not acknowledged. But wavering between reference to ordinary language and a not-fully-conscious use of modern scientific discourse, theology speaks of "facts" or "events" of salvation in an epistemologically uncontrolled sense. I do not mean that the corresponding experience of faith, the apostolic testimony that has come down to us, does not have its own precise consistency; I mean that its translation into the language of modernity is still lacking, precisely because theology has always tried to avoid completely the scientific notion of historical factuality (since the object, God Himself, cannot be contained within it) or to take it simply as a given element without evaluating its capacity (which may even be minimal) to comprehend the elements of faith.

The historical-theoretical reflection that follows is an inquiry into how this question — the hermeneutical question— was experienced in the Protestant and modernist discussion at the end of the nineteenth and beginning of the twentieth century: we arrive at no definitive solutions, of course, but we do acquire greater insight into matters that until then had remained in the shadows. My thanks go to all those philosophers and theologians, who through their conversations or their books have helped shape this work, in particular E. Poulat, G. Penzo, G. Ruggieri, S. Dianich, P.C. Bori, A. Rizzi, P. Boschini, M. Fini, M. Pesce, S. Sorrentino; of course, responsibility for the final form of the book must remain my own.

This book was conceived as a whole, though some parts of it have been already published. In particular, chapter V appeared in no. 1 (1991) of the review *Filosofia e teologia* dedicated to the topic "The Essence of Christianity and History" (contributions by Dianich, Sorrentino, Boschini, Forni, Cerrato, Gallas, Bof); chapter VI is the introduction to the work *Storia e dogma*, by M. Blondel, Italian translation by G. Forni (Brescia: Queriniana, 1992). The Appendix appeared in the review *Cristianesimo nella storia*, no. 12 (Bologna: EDB, 1991).

ABBREVIATIONS

AC *The Absoluteness of Christianity and the History of Religions*
E. Troeltsch

BS *A.Loisy entre la foi et l'incroyance* R.de Boyer de Sainte Suzanne

CCM *Au coeur de la crise moderniste* ed. R.Marlé

CM *Critique et mystique* E.Poulat

DP *Das Problem der Religion* W.Dilthey

EE *L'Evangile et l'Eglise* A.Loisy

GC *The Gospel and the Church* A.Loisy

HDC *Histoire, dogme et critique dans la crise moderniste* E.Poulat

MR *The Two Sources of Morality and Religion* H.Bergson

PE *Les premiers écrits de M.Blondel* M.Blondel

PL *Autour d'un petit livre* A.Loisy

PR *Outlines of a Philosophy of Religion based on Psychology and History*
A.Sabatier

RM *Y a-t-il deux sources de la religion et de la morale?* A.Loisy

SL *Un clerc qui n'a pas trahi* S.Leblanc (H.Bremond)

TB *G.Tyrrell et H.Bremond* A.Loisy

UR *Über die Religion* F.Schleiermacher

WC *What is Christianity?* A.Harnack

WH *Was heisst 'Wesen des Christentums?'* E.Troeltsch

I

The Liberal Evolutionism of Auguste Sabatier

Already from the title of his major work *Outlines of a Philosophy of Religion based on Psychology and History*[1] we can understand the fundamental intention of this important exponent of French Protestantism: to reconcile Christianity and history, within the context of a general acceptance of the new secular culture. Like other authors we shall be seeing later, in particular Harnack and Loisy, Sabatier means in his research to adhere exclusively to the scientific method (which, together with moral values, sums up the ideals of the century[2]) but this does not prevent a precise philosophy of history from emerging in his work, as it does in that of the others; the history of Christianity is above all a progress, which can be expressed in various ways and has many meanings. "This volume contains three parts which are related to each other as the three stories of one and the same edifice. The first treats of religion and its origin; the second of Christianity and its essence; the third of dogma and its nature. Proceeding thus from the general to the particular, from the elementary forms of religion to its highest form, passing afterwards from religious phenomena to religious doctrines, to their formation and to the laws that determine them, I have endeavoured to develop a series of connected and progressive views which I do not wish to be regarded as a system, but as the rigid application and the first results of the method of strict psychological and historical observation that

---

[1] *Esquisse d'une philosophie de la religion d'après la psychologie et l'histoire* (Paris: Fischbacher, 1897); photostatic reprint of original edition, with the abbreviated title *Esquisse d'une philosophie de la religion* and an introduction by G. Puaux (Paris: Fischbacher, 1969). English translation by T.A. Seed (New York: Harper, 1957) (referred to henceforth with the abbreviation PR). Among the few studies on Sabatier we refer the reader to that of B. Reymond, *Le procès de l'autorité dans la théologie d'A.S.* (Lausanne: L'Age de l'Homme, 1976) (with bibliography, pp. 307-27).

[2] PR, p. xi.

for years I have applied to this species of studies".[3]

Clearly, the movement that is perceived towards the particular, the specified, and at the same time upwards, goes well beyond what is offered by mere "observation"; it is a philosophy of history that, as in the hegelian perspective, brings historical development closer to the evolution of thought, except that here the final outcome does not seem to be philosophy, the universal conceptual element, but a particular religious formation that in a certain sense has left behind it the philosophical generalities about religion.

Indeed, if, as we said, the "two great passions" of the century are the scientific method and the moral ideal, to conform to the times will also mean to present Christianity essentially as a *morality* (which is by no means difficult after Kant and the neo-kantian elaborations of the second half of the nineteenth century), and at the same time to prove "scientifically" (that is, historically) that this presentation is correct. There is, however, a third element that is another great passion of the century and reappears everywhere: it is the philosophy of history, evolutionism, which makes it possible to see this moral or interior Christianity as something that arrives last, after Catholicism, and that is, as it were, a purification of it. From the very first pages Sabatier wants to make clear the meaning of his evolutionism, which some people had criticised as being naturalism: "The first reproach made against me is contained in the words 'naturalist evolutionism', with which some have thought fit to define my doctrine. In this way I am attributed with a more or less materialistic conception of the universe according to which I am said to explain everything solely with the law of evolution, as Spencer does, and sooner or later I should end up making the laws of the moral world dependent on the laws of the physical world since I make the former simply a transformation of the latter. Do I need to say that this is the opposite of what I think? I do not directly propose any metaphysical conception but if anyone wished to find one in this book, I think a completely opposite one would be apparent".

By opposite conception Sabatier has in mind a system in which "moral life is born slowly and painfully out of organic life", but cannot be reduced simply to this; on the contrary, the method adopted makes it possible to see "that there is a movement forwards, real progress from one to the other, that the first in time has its purpose in the second, that there is a kind of living, continuous creation of which every stage manifests new

---

[3] PR, p. xi.

wealth and glories".[4]

But a spiritualistic evolutionism of this kind also has the advantage of reconciling faith and science. "The opposition, established by Scholasticism, between faith and science is it not as irreligious as it is irrational and has it not been one of the chief causes of the death of theology in the Church and of the triumph of incredulity in the secular world? While developing along parallel lines, can science and faith remain isolated? Man is one, and his scientific activity, like his religious activity, tends to a synthesis. The synthesis will be found in a teleological consideration of the universe". This is because, essentially, it is science that has taken us from a mechanistic conception of nature, in which miracle appeared as infraction, to a vitalistic or evolutionistic conception, in which nature is constantly creating new forms: everything is a miracle and nothing is. "The theory of the ascensional evolution of beings, which renders miracle useless, shows nature to us in the course of constant transformation and perpetual travail... Cosmic evolution proceeds always from that which is poorer to that which is richer, from the simple to the complex, from the homogeneous to the heterogeneous, from dead matter to living matter, from physical to spiritual life. At each stage nature surpasses itself by a mysterious creation that resembles a true miracle in relation to an inferior stage". Is this an act of nature or of God? Of nature above all, of its "hidden force" but faith will always be able to see in it a higher finalism and a divine action and so it will continue to believe what the old notion of miracle presumed: "the real and active presence of God, the answer to prayer and the liberty to hope".[5] Sabatier interpreted historical development in an optimistic sense, as a maturing that is neither mechanincal nor biological or social; in its highest phases it requires the mediation of masters or inspired guides,[6] and is always an individual realisation, a faithfulness to God often consciously directed against the idolatry and immorality of the masses; there is no

---

4   PR, pp. VI-VIII in French edition. Omitted in the translation by Seed. Translated by the translator. Cf. also pp. 118-120.

5   PR, pp. 79-83.

6   Cf. the same need in Schleiermacher regarding prophetism: *Über die Religion. Reden an die Gebildeten unter ihren Verächtern*, edited by H.J. Rothert (Hamburg: Meiner, 1958) (cited henceforth with the initials UR) p. 5; English translation by John Oman, *On Religion: Speeches to its Cultured Despisers*, 1958.(New York: Harper and Row), p.5. For the relationship between Sabatier and Schleiermacher see B. Reymond, "Comment les francophones ont-ils lu et compris Schleiermacher avant 1914?", *Archivio di filosofia*, LII:1-3 (1984) pp. 465-97 (with bibliography, pp. 489-97).

fatality or necessity that takes a process of growth this far, but only the free, responsible creativity of a few men, who are often in conflict with all the others. It should not therefore be said that this is "the work of time and Nature, unless you see God at work in time, and, beneath this word Nature, by the side of realised and manifested forces you perceive the hidden and immeasurable virtualities which ferment in it and carry it beyond itself into the higher life of liberty and love".[7]

If the religious evolution of humanity moves in the direction of the interiorisation and moralisation of beliefs and thus comes closer to the modern scientific consciousness, Protestantism is the fulfilment of Catholicism in that it eliminates all material or crudely mythological elements from it and attempts a critical understanding of it: "Before any *a priori* definition or deduction I take note of what psychological and historical observation actually gives me". For example, in the case of original sin, observation tells me that in every one of us sin is inevitable, due to natural and environmental conditionings that are outside our control, and also that, paradoxically, we percieve its origin dependent on our will and therefore our responsibility. Why should it be any different for the first man? Why should we suppose a state of initial perfection from which man strayed? "In order to solve the mystery of the origin of evil there is no point going back to a past that remains inaccessible to us, and resort either to the purely mythical hypothesis of the fall of the first human couple, who were supposed to have lived in a kind of golden age, or to the metaphysical hypothesis of a pre-existential fall that has no foundation in psychology and puts off the problem *ad infinitum*, without solving it". Sabatier defends himself from his critics (who accused him of "insulting divine justice", evidently because, if evil exists from the origins it must stem from God) saying that they make no effort to understand "the development of moral life only using the positive data of psychology and history".[8]

But Sabatier's philosophy of history, though influenced by Hegel and Spencer, paradoxically always affirms a certain unitary design of human evolution, but at the same time asserts that life or experience are the ultimate foundation. In this way the philosophy of history in a certain sense annuls itself since if its aim is interior and subjective it cannot but end up in an indefinite multiplication of individual points of view: "But,

---

7 PR, pp. 120-21.

8 PR, pp. IX-XII in French edition. Omitted in Seed's translation. Translation of translator.

however exhaustive my explanations are, I can do no other here than make an interior, personal confession. I do not think that the problem in question, the terms of which are essentially subjective and vary from individual to individual, can possibly have a uniform and dogmatic solution that anyone can or should receive from the outside".[9] The Christian God is an "interior God" and we would search for Him in vain outside of ourselves; and of course, in this interiorisaton we must see, apart from the memory of St. Augustine, the modern traits of the Protestant hermeneutic consciousness, the demythologisation (psychologisation or moralisation) of beliefs, the reference to experience as sufficient basis for an authentic religiosity, the philosophical-scientific transcription of Christianity as a positive alternative after the collapse of the great metaphysical or dogmatic constructions. Catholicism, on the contrary, is an exterior, authoritarian religion; it is the continuation of the Roman Empire by other means. In fact, what did the word "religion" mean in Rome? "Instead of marking the inward and subjective side of religion, and signalising it as a phenomenon of the life of the soul, it defined religion by the outside, as a tradition of rites, and as a social institution bequeathed by ancestors... Such is the form under which the genius of Rome conceived and realised Christianity in the Western world".[10] Catholicism, precisely because it is a "political and social conception of religion", has given unilateral emphasis to the intellectual, cognitive aspect, "but this intellectual element, however indispensable, so far from being the basis and the substance of religion, varies continually at all the epochs of religious evolution. Doctrinal formulas and liturgies are means of expression and of education, of which religion avails itself, but which it can exchange for others after each philosophical crisis. Rites and beliefs become obliterated or die out; religion possesses a power of perpetual resurrection, whose principle cannot be exhausted in any external form or in any dogmatic idea".[11]

But with this radical historicisation or relativisation that considers the doctrines or dogmas as the external covering of a more secret nucleus, as the limited expression of a life that constantly goes beyond it (here Sabatier again bases himself on Schleiermacher), what is left as the essence of religion or of Christianity? We do not yet know, but we do know that the solution will have to be sought in the direction of the ethical individualism that his philosophy of history leads to and, in this sense, in

---

[9] PR, p. 5 in French edition. Omitted in Seed's translation. Translation of translator.
[10] PR, p. 3.
[11] PR, p. 6.

the realm of experience and not of science. "The question man puts to himself in religion is always a question of salvation, and if he seems sometimes to be pursuing in it the enigma of the universe, it is only that he may solve the enigma of his life". Here the existential and confession-like tones we have already mentioned reappear but the opposition that had been developing between knowledge and life, exterior and interior, authority and freedom, seems to be moving towards an ethical-practical dissolution or vanification (individualistic or pragmatic) of every possible truth. But was the point of the psychological-historical transcription of Christianity to renew its image in contact with the modern world, or was it to designate as Christian any interiority that, when times are mature, a person feels or experiences as his religion?[12]

Echoing Schleiermacher, Sabatier begins by defining religion, following the general outline in three parts presented at the beginning of his book; he continues with a definition of Christianity and of dogma. This work on the "essence" was necessary, in the approach of Sabatier and Harnack, because they were starting out from the modern historical consciousness and therefore from the awareness that traditional presentations, whether Catholic or Protestant, had been destroyed by illuministic criticism or they were inadequate for the nineteenth-century development of the anthropological sciences. Sabatier takes up Schleiermacher's idea of a double movement, inwards and outwards, that governs the life of man, and indeed of every organism in general, but he draws conclusions of an ethical or existential nature that have nothing to do with Schleiermacher. "From the beginning the life of the psyche implies

---

[12] Cf. PR, p. 11. The democratic concepts of illuministic and romantic derivation (the supremacy of individual intuition and feeling) radically transformed the theory of interpretation, and were the foundation, especially with Schleiermacher, of modern hermeneutics. In opposition to the transcendency of the giuridic norm or the theological assertion, which I try to understand as something beyond the reach of my will and having a superior life, there comes into play the psychological, sociological or historical immanence of every truth; this in fact is formed in dialogue, friendship and social relations, and only in this way, inasmuch as it is experienced directly by us, is it present as truth. Dilthey did little more than draw the conclusions of an age-old question (that went back to Pietist religiosity, Rousseau and Goethe) when he insisted on the concept of *Erlebnis* as the basis of understanding; this has certainly meant for modern Christianity that faith is faithfulness, that is, *life* according to the will of the Father, which allows us to understand it; but it has also meant (at least since Rousseau) that imaginative or emotional immediacy constitutes and legitimately forms our religion.

a double movement: a movement inward from the outside to the centre of the ego, and a movement outward from the centre to the circumference. The first represents the action of external things upon the ego by sensation (passivity); the second, the reaction of the ego upon things by the will (activity)".[13] Sabatier fails to grasp the hermeneutic implications of the romantic metaphysics present in the *Speeches*, for example the fact that Schleiermacher aims at an interpenetration or a balance between the two movements, and certainly not at the prevailing of one over the other (he speaks in negative terms of those who "find themselves at the extremes", who live almost exclusively in a single direction);[14] Schleiermacher too relativises the historical expressions of religion and turns to religious experience, to the relation between finite and infinite that is at the basis of every experience and manifestation of the divine, but he is a long way from setting the creativity of life in opposition to cognitive mediation. Sabatier does not see this side of the problem and interprets the double movement as a conflict out of which consciousness arises: "This perpetual collision, this conflict of the ego and the universe, — this is the primary cause and origin of all pain. Thus thrown back upon itself, the activity of the ego returns upon the centre and heats it like the axle of a wheel in motion. Sparks soon fly, and the inner life of the ego is lit up. This is *consciousness*".[15] Sabatier also recalls Schleiermacher's definition of religion as a "feeling of dependence", but he deems it necessary to modify it adding an active element, which is prayer: "This concrete definition of religion has the advantage of correcting by completing that of Schleiermacher. It reconciles the two antithetic elements which constitute the religious sentiment: the passive and the active elements, the feeling of dependence and the movement of liberty... Schleiermacher erred in insisting only upon resignation. Thenceforth he could neither escape Pantheism in order to arrive at liberty, nor find any link between the religious and the moral life".[16]

A little ahead of Troeltsch (*The Absoluteness of Christianity and the*

---

13 PR, pp. 12-13. Cf. F. Schleiermacher, *Über Die Religion*, cit., I. Rede: "Apologie" (UR, pp. 1-21).

14 Cf. G. Forni, *Studi di ermeneutica. Schleiermacher, Dilthey, Cassirer* (Bologna: Clueb, 1985) chapter I: "'Quelli che si trovano agli estremi'. La psicologia romantica nell' 'Apologia' di Schleiermacher", pp. 17-41.

15 PR, pp. 13.

16 PR, pp. 26-27, 29. In the bibliographical note to chapter I the only work of Schleiermacher that Sabatier mentions is the *Speeches* of 1799 (p. 30 in French edition. Omitted in English translation).

History of Religions, 1902), Sabatier next deals with the concept of revelation in a way that does not compromise the positive evaluation of non-Christian religions (there is revelation, the "positive manifestation" of God wherever there is religion) and does link it to particular events or moments in history ("Revelation is not a communication once and for all of immutable doctrines").[17] Rather, in contrast with the Catholic conception of a revelation that has already taken place, in Sabatier there is a sense of expectancy, as there is in Troeltsch; Nature and the world contain within them "a hidden force, an incommensurable *potential energy*, an ever open, never exhausted fount of apparitions at once magnificent and unexpected"; if all this holds for miracles it must hold too for revelation which extends into the present and into the future.[18] Since in reality God always acts in a progressive way and the history of Israel is characterised by "moral and religious progress", for us too revelation will have the sense of a "creation, a purification and progressive clearness of the consciousness of God in each individual and in humanity", passing through three phases: "the mythological, the dogmatic and the critical".[19] Fundamentally, man always begins from an infantile state in which the imagination, the mythical and symbolic consciousness, prevails; but then, as St. Paul says, we abandon the thoughts and speech of the child. At the beginning mankind does not distinguish the substance and the form of his beliefs; later he does, and we would not be able to confront the texts of the ancient religions without criticism and translation. Primitive and ancient peoples took natural phenomena to be signs of the divine will, but even this religious naturalism (which in fact continues to exist, in a more subtle form, in the exterior or in some way physical conceptions of revelation) was later abandoned. There was thus a great progress, that occurred above all in Israel: revelation became interior and moral, its limit being that the action of God in man came to be seen as a kind of magical possession or it was mistaken for mental illness. With Christ, revelation becomes something more intimate to man; it loses its more infantilely mythological characteristics connected with naturalism,

---

[17] PR, p. 33. Cf. E. Troeltsch, *Die Absolutheit des Christentums und die Religionsgeschichte* (Tübingen: Mohr, 1902, 1929³); translated into English by David Reid (London: SCM Press, 1972) (abbreviation AC).

[18] Cf. PR, p. 82. On the theme of a "religion of the future" in the philosophical thought of the period, and especially in Positivism, see E. Poulat, *Critique et mystique. Autour de Loisy ou la conscience catholique et l'esprit moderne* (Paris: Ed. du Centurion, 1984), chapter VII: "Nouveaux christianismes et religion de l'humanité", pp. 217-53 (henceforth CM).

[19] Cf. pp. VIII-IX of French edition, PR, pp. 33-34, 120.

it also loses any exceptional, violent or miraculous characteristic of divine intervention and it is normalised as pure interiority and moral life. But Catholicism was looking for a foundation for authority and found it in the concept of external revelation: in a doctrine which was legitimized (Greek rationalism) or sustained (Judaistic supernaturalism) by miracles. In opposition to this conception Sabatier refers back his criticism of scholastic intellectualism, to the weakness of the supposed proofs and lastly to the historical-critical problem posed by the Scriptures: the Bible is neither simply revelation nor can it be said that its every word is inspired by God.[20]

There is then a third phase, which Sabatier calls "critical" or "psychological" and with which he clearly identifies; it conceives of revelation as "evident, interior and progressive", in the sense that to insist on evidence must always preclude a material or external conception of divine signs (in this sense miracles do not prove anything and they do not even appear as miracles except to the believing consciousness) and must at the same time actualise the religious message as something that extends into our life in a real way. "Listen: only one criterion is sufficient and infallible: every divine revelation, every religious experience fit to nourish and sustain your soul, must be able to repeat and continue itself as an actual revelation and an individual experience in your own consciousness... The revelations of the past are efficacious and real if they render you fit to receive the personal revelation that God reserves for you... The aim of tradition is liberty, and liberty returns lovingly to tradition when, instead of finding it a yoke, it sees in it only help, nourishment and light".[21]

Although Sabatier rejects the Catholic conception of miracle as a demonstration, he does not seem to want to attribute it exclusively to an interior transformation: a miracle is something real for the believing consciousness, even in a physical sense; indeed these two sides of the problem should not be separated: "the distinction sometimes made between the *manifestation* of God in things and divine *inspiration* in consciousness, between the sign or external miracle and the inward word, is of little worth... The manifestation of God in nature or in history is always a matter of faith".[22] However, in the following pages, the recognition of a miracle seems to be dependent only on the "critical observation", i.e. scientific observation, of the facts; and in any case progress (but not just scientific progress, also the *religious* progress that God Himself is constantly introducing into the

---

[20] PR, pp. 35-52.

[21] PR, pp. 52-54, 60-61.

[22] PR, p. 53.

history of mankind, and which is essentially in accord with scientific progress) leads to a demythologisaton, to a reduction of the miraculous element. "Far from being more striking or more numerous, miracles and prodigies in the Bible are rarer than elsewhere, clearer, less fantastic, more under law to conscience and to common sense".[23] What Sabatier wants to show right from the start is that in Judaism and then in Christianity (unlike in other ancient religions) with regard to miracles there existed a prudence, a sobriety, or even a devalorisation and transformation into a different element, which Sabatier calls ethical; thus Christianity is a religion of antiquity that has its true destiny, its true realisation, in the modern world, in which these conceptions also belong to the field of philosophy, and thus a particular convergence of Christianity and secular culture is created. The "superiority" of the Jewish prophets over the pagan seers lies "in a purer idea of God; in a higher ideal of justice, in a religion that is essentially moral"; they put their trust "on the one hand in the sovranity of their God and on the other in the inflexible law of moral conscience". Even the prophecies of John the Baptist, or of Christ Himself, "in no way come from a special gift or from a miraculous divining power, but from a firmer moral conviction, from a more profound life in God, from a more sincere and disinterested piety... The moral notion of prophecy remains, but the notion of miracle has gone".[24]

The history of religions shows the progress of religious consciousness and of the conception of the divine: from particularity to universality, from multiplicity to unity, from uniformity to differentiation, from exteriority to interiority and from matter to spirit.[25] And in this process Christianity appears as a perfect religion in that it coincides with a moral human life of a superior kind. "In the religion of Jesus there is nothing religious but that which is authentically moral, and nothing moral in human life that is not truly religious. The perfect religion coincides with the absolute morality, and this naturally extends to and is obligatory on all mankind... We find that the religious and the human ideals join, no more to be separated and that humanity, having begun in man (still) animal, with the grossest form of religion,achieves full realisation in the perfect religion".[26] Clearly, this identification, this reconciliation of heaven and earth, of the divine and the human was only a presage and a long process of education, willed by

---

[23] PR, p. 66, 70.

[24] PR, p. 94-95 in French edition. Omitted in English translation.

[25] PR, pp. 93 ff.

[26] PR, pp. 99-100.

God Himself, was necessary for it to appear in full light: "religion and morality were destined to approach each other and to penetrate each other more and more, until the perfect religion should be recognised by this sign: the highest piety under the form of the ideal morality. At bottom Christianity has no other principle, and it is for this reason more than any other that it is not only the highest form of religion, but the universal and final religion".[27] Thus, in Sabatier's thought there appears not only the final outcome of a certain individualisation and progressive secularisation of Christianity (an outcome that, with no precise coherence, is sometimes reduced to a historical-evolutionary factor of a higher gaining of awareness of the interior, universal nature of the moral law); there appears also that this process is a necessary development, and this seems to emerge from the historical, or historical-philosophical studies of the essential stages of religious evolution. "Between the religion of the prophets and the religion of Jesus, however, there is one more barrier to be broken down. In the 'Kingdom of God', the idea of nation must give place to the idea of humanity. The universal God must be represented as the immanent God, as present in every human soul, without difference or distinction... A supreme crisis was necessary, so that the pure diamond could emerge out of the shattered block. The Hebrew nation must perish, totally and with no hope of return, so that, from under the Hebrew exterior, the human conscience might finally appear, free and naked before God".[28]

In the second book of his work of 1897 Sabatier has given us a more specific reflection on Christianity that anticipates Harnack's concept of an "essence of Christianity". This "essence", "principle" or "root" is seen not from the point of view of a church — as then we would be entering on an "interminable debate" — but from the point of view of psychology and history, in other words, of science. "Essence" must be taken to mean a perfect relationship with God, which presents itself in the inner experience of the Christian, and a historical foundation for this relationship in Christ, in his person and in his spirit. "Christianity is therefore not only the ideal, but a historical religion, inseparably connected not only with the maxims of morality and the truths of the doctrine of Jesus, but with His person itself, and with the permanent action of the new spirit that animated Him, and which lives from generation to generation in His disciples". The main theological problem thus seems to Sabatier to be to unite the absolute and universal nature of Christianity with its historicity; in fact, it is "in history"

----

[27] PR, p. 110.
[28] PR, p. 129.

that Christianity is present "as the final crowning of the religious evolution of humanity" and "perfect religion". But this union or reconciliation is not possible with an intellectualistic or metaphysical conception, in a Catholic sense: "In making of Christ the Second Person of the Eternal Trinity, the Son of the Father, consubstantial and equal, it removes Him from history and transports Him into metaphysics. But thus to deify history is also a way to destroy it. The dogma annuls the limited, contingent, and human character of the appearance of Jesus of Nazareth. His life loses all reality... We have only a deity walking in the midst of His contemporaries, hidden beneath a human figure".[29]

To put it more simply, the mistake of the intellectualistic conception (of theological rationalism or of Catholic metaphysics) is to conceive of the "essence" as the truths and dogmas, whereas it is entirely in the filial relationship which, from Christ onwards and following His example, we have with a God who is Father. The religious consciousness of Jesus is the "fountain-head" of this experience of sonship, and therefore of the essence of Christianity, and in this way Sabatier believes he has found the solution to the problem that worried him: "On the one hand, Christianity, by this filial union with God, is seen to be the ideal and perfect religion; on the other, it appears as a real fact in the consciousness of Jesus Christ, so that this religious reality comes to us with the imperative character of the ideal".[30]

It may be that Sabatier was influenced by Hegel because the reconciliation of real and ideal, of human and divine appears to him as an insuperable conclusion: "Is not religious evolution accomplished when these two terms, God and man, opposed to each other at the origin of conscious life on earth, interpenetrate each other till they reach the moral unity of love, in which God becomes interior to man and lives in him, in which man becomes interior to God and finds in God the full expansion of his being? Christianity is therefore the absolute and final religion of mankind". Seen in this perspective Christianity is a historical-evolutionary factor of prime importance, which leads man to a higher life but presents nothing that is not a perfecting of human life on this earth. It is here that its non-abstract, non-doctrinal nature can be seen: in the consciousness of Jesus there is a new *life*, a life, moreover, that is observable by means of historical science; a life that, from an evolutionary point of view, can be compared to the progress from animality to humanity and that on earth realises: "the

---

[29] PR, pp. 135-37.
[30] PR, pp. 143-46.

kingdom of God, that is, of free, pure spirit, of righteousness and love".[31] Of course, in order to work in this direction it is also necessary to reduce or translate the ecclesial heredity (especially the biblical heredity), and it is here that we find ourselves nearest to the roots of Sabatier's hermeneutical approach: the importance of the historical sciences of religion, in their modern (critical-illuministic) use, lies in the fact that their procedure is one that demythologises, that translates miraculous or prodigious occurrences into their *ethical* substance or that shows the irrelevance of many historical accounts and situations for the definition of the essence, of the stable or permanent nucleus. And, as has been seen, this nucleus will be identified in the real experience, which can always exist anew, of the fundamental relationship with God and not in what old documents or memories of the past tell us. (Schleiermacher, in fact, thought that the truly religious man did not need a sacred text but could write one himself).[32] In short, to be a Christian, or to believe that Christianity is "the perfect religion", there is no need to "take the whole Gospel story to be true", as if "the tradition or the legend about Christ were really the essence of Christianity. We have found this essence in a religious experience, in an inner revelation of God that operated for the first time in the soul of Jesus of Nazareth, but which occurs and repeats itself, albeit less luminous, but not unrecognisable, in the soul of all his true disciples. As a result of this, the Christian principle is not a memory of the past, or a dead doctrine enclosed in a document, but it is something ever alive that is transmitted through Christian life itself, and is thus present in all times and contemporary to all generations".[33] Sabatier thus emphasises the practical, and potentially relativistic, principle (for who are the "true" disciples if the only criterion of truth is experience?) that was already present in Schleiermacher and in the pietist groups, about which Dilthey wrote in *The Problem of Religion* (1911): "Religious truth is no longer ultimately to be found in the testimony of the Scriptures, but in real experience... Intellectual religious knowledge is placed after the process that grows up within the life of the psyche as a whole and it springs from that life".[34]

Historical criticism cannot corrode the ethical nucleus of Christianity,

---

31 PR, pp. 146-47. Cf. also pp. 152-53, 159-60.

32 Cf. F. Schleiermacher, UR, p. 68.

33 PR, pp. 187-88 in French edition. Omitted in Seed's translation. Translator's translation.

34 Cf. W. Dilthey, "Das Problem der Religion", in *Gesammelte Schriften*, VI (Leipzig-Berlin: Teubner, 1924), p. 292 (abbreviation DP).

but it can corrode all its various metaphysical interpretations. Concerning the first point, however much we praise this science and practice it "in order to free the positive human reality from the mythological legends that always get mixed in with the old stories", it will never be able to do anything against "the moral value of the Christian principle", because here all that counts is the religious consciousness. And certainly, as history progresses we are able to distinguish better between the substance and the exterior forms of Christianity, between the fundamental religious consciousness and its numerous expressions: the former can be scientifically verified but it is also a universal human element; the latter are the product of poetic or speculative imagination and belong to particular historical contexts. "Here it is important to prevent a misunderstanding and avoid confusing or identifying the psychological phenomenon, the inner, living fact of piety that we saw in the soul of Christ, with the theological explanations, and with the dogma that have resulted from them. Whereas the fact of consciousness is one, the explanations and dogma are various". So, while at the beginning the divine Sonship of Christ was spoken of in connection with his being the Messiah, because it was normal to call a descendant of David god or son of god, later recourse was made to the "popular and pious legend" of the virgin birth and to the idea of the pre-existence of Christ before his birth on earth; his birth had by this time become an incarnation and "the ecclesiastical dogma of the divinity of Jesus" had been established. But, according to Sabatier, in this way the humanity of Jesus becomes a deceptive appearance, and the unity between God and man, which was the main feature of Christianity and was what made it the perfect religion, is once again lost: "I find myself in a form of refined, higher paganism, in the presence of a Christianity that in the guise of transcendental metaphysics is nothing but new mythology".[35]

The universality of Christianity is thus not metaphysical, but moral and scientific. It is moral because one of the important aspects of the teaching of Jesus is the absence of theory and at the same time the understanding of man in his existentially most profound nature: "Christ did not construct a theory of man, of his moral life, any more than he constructed a theory with respect to God and the universe. He was content to place himself at the centre of the human consciousness, and to dig down to the source of life. He takes man as he is in all climates and in all conditions". But this universality also has a scientific significance, because only the modern historical consciousness allows us to distinguish between

---

[35] PR, pp. 188-92 in French edition. Omitted in Seed's translation. Translator's translation.

"the purely moral essence of Christianity" and its "historical expressions or realisations". This distinction should be applied not only to the dogmas of the various churches, but also to the Bible (in that a distinction must be made "between the word of God and its human and historical expression") and to the Gospel (the teaching of Jesus has "an oriental and contingent form which needs to be translated into our modern languages").[36]

But the essence also represents a *critical* or normative instance (because it says what is acceptable or is not acceptable in the single manifestations), as well as an *origin* to start out from or a *goal* to arrive at - which again calls into play a certain philosophy of history; and it is well-known that from its origins in the eighteenth century the philosophy of history has made use of biological images like the development or growth of humanity (the life of which is compared to the course of a single life in Herder and Rousseau).[37] So it can be seen that there is a complex theoretical situation deriving from the notion of organism being applied to history: for Sabatier, it is naturally not a question of justifying every possible manifestation for, as we know, there is a progress in history; but we have to recognise (here too, in opposition to an objectivistic and Catholic conception of truth) that we can grasp the absolute only in the relative, historical form, the essence in the manifestation, and that this mediated or hermeneutical characteristic of religious experience is not only unavoidable, but is willed by God: "Jesus wished to force his hearers to interpret His words, because He called them to an inward, personal and autonomous activity, because He wished to put an end to the religion of the letter and of rites and to found the religion of the spirit. Even now, he that does not give himself to this labour of interpretation and assimilation in reading the Gospel... cannot understand or profit by His teaching".[38]

---

[36] PR, pp. 158, 160-61.

[37] The concepts of development or growth, of the organism that assimilates material from outside itself to make it its own, and also the image, already present in the Gospels, of the seed and the tree can be found to be dominant in three areas: hermeneutics — the philosophy of history — the interpretation of Christianity. These concepts derive from German Romanticism and provide the dawning historicism with the means of combating the Enlightenment and the Revolution (biology against physics, organism against mechanism); they are present in the hermeneutical theories of Schleiermacher, Nietzsche and Dilthey (and it is this which, despite the underlying opposition, pointed out many times by Dilthey himself, between the individualism of Nietzsche and Dilthey's theory of "culture", links them both to the romantic inheritance).

[38] PR, p. 149.

It is clear that there will be a variable relation between the essence and its manifestations, of greater or lesser faithfulness, according to the historical period and the historical development. And here too we encounter various problems, because, for example, it is not clear whether the essence is a goal, a conclusion, or also an origin, a beginning; whether the essence effectively reaches us in a religious experience here and now, given that this experience is inevitably mediated and that we only ever encounter religious manifestations, or expressions; whether reference to the life or experience of the individual may not operate as a criterion of individualistic dissemination, reinforced by the prevailingly practical nature of truth, which would make it impossible to establish any univocal essence, etc. In fact, it is difficult to know what Christianity is if it is at once "an ideal which is never reached and an inner force which ever urges us beyond ourselves"; but for Sabatier truth coincides with freedom and with that interior and spiritual movement that frees us from the chains of the past. In this way he is obliged to place this philosophical Christianity at the beginning of the process and to see the struggle that follows as a struggle for freedom from metaphysical or dogmatic backsliding: "Finally, I see on what condition Christianity may remain faithful to itself while realising itself in history. It is only by an incessant struggle of the Christian principle against all the elements of the past which find, alas, in human propensities, and in the inertia of the multitude, a complicity so constant and effectual... To cease to fight is to succumb; it is to allow yourself to be submerged in the rising tide of human superstitions; it is to die. What is the flame when it burns no more? Who does not see the danger of allowing Christianity to become absorbed in one Church form, Christian truth in one formula, the Christian principle in one of its particular realisations?".[39]

Sabatier has stressed interpretative mediation and the individual nature of interpretation, he has affirmed, with vitalistic or idealistic expressions, the "spiritual" — interior and free in the sense of German Protestantism — overcoming of every false objectivation, of every bond or doctrine (it is precisely here, in Protestantism, that the spirit "becomes conscious of self"[40]); but he has still to account for the relationship between what changes and what remains the same, and he does so assuming that the essence or the origin can be spoken of as one, as of a germ out of which grows the tree: "The distinction between the Christian principle and its successive realisations renders it easy to resolve the question, formerly so

---

[39] PR, pp. 165, 171-72.
[40] PR, p. 215.

much debated, as to the perfectibility of Christianity. It is clear that, considered in its internal and ideal principle, it is not perfectible. It is perfect piety, plenary union with God, consequently the absolute and definitive religion. But, regarded in its historical evolution, not only is it perfectible, but it must ceaselessly progress, since, for it, to progress is to realise itself. The germ could not be perfected in its essence, as germ and ideal type of the tree that it potentially contains. But the tree itself only comes into existence by the development of the germ".[41]

In Sabatier's opinion, this position allows the "Christian thinker" to maintain "a truly historical point of view" and to reconcile truth and charity, which is still necessary with regard to the various manifestations of Christianity even if we already know the spiritual evolution of mankind and the significance of its basic phases: Hebraism, Catholicism and Protestantism.[42] However, he wishes to disassociate himself from a Protestant conception of the first Judaic period, which tends to consider this Christianity as the "ideal and abstract" model — because it was inspired directly by God — which every age should attempt to reproduce, and as the "first chapter of the history of Protestantism": "By dissipating these prejudices, historical criticism has completely resuscitated that first form of Christianity. It is no longer possible to confound it with any other". Clearly here we have a difficult problem since the essence that appears at the end as the sense and direction of the process must also be there at the beginning, it must be the Christianity of Jesus. We shall see also in other writers — especially in Harnack — the difficulty and tension that this theoretical situation creates because it involves saying that modern Christianity, which is moral and interior, is that of the origins; in other words, that the "essential" Christianity we are arriving at is primitive Christianity itself, after the immense deviation of Catholicism. Not even Sabatier can escape from this typically Protestant approach; he too, speaking of essence or principle, necessarily speaks also of a pure, spiritual, interior origin (the Christianity of Jesus) which is then put forward as the goal of the historical process. Thus, his need, illustrated in the passage quoted, to recognise the specificity of that early Christianity must restrict itself to considering the principle at the beginning mixed with non-essential Jewish elements (the diamond, still hidden in the rock); later history would realise the principle through a process of progressive purification. In this sense, in early Christianity the "soul" (the essence, the nucleus) can be thought

---

[41] PR, p. 173.
[42] PR, pp. 174-77.

of as new and the "body" (the non-essential covering, the husk) as old, that is, of Jewish derivation: "In this first form of Christianity... there was a certain dualism, a mixture of heterogeneous and soon hostile elements. The struggle was bound to arise between the Christian tradition and Jewish tradition. The new seed sown in that ancient soil could not germinate without rising in it and in places breaking up the thick hard crust. In the books of the New Testament that have preserved for us the picture of that first and powerful germination, side by side with the principle to which belongs the future we necessarily find old things which are on the way to death. It will be seen what an error they commit and what a wrong they do themselves who, misconceiving this historical complexity, sanctify and deify both these opposite elements, and place on the same level the eternally fruitful grain, and the chaff today dried up and inert, a mere remnant of the Jewish stalk that bore it".[43]

If it was just a stalk to be discarded the matter would be quite simple; but Sabatier knows that between the grain and the chaff there is the same relation of mediation or incorporation that exists between the essence and its manifestations. What, after all, is primitive Christianity if not the Jewish expression of an eternal principle? But, in that case, between the elements indicated there cannot be only conflict, but also a positive relation of manifestation, of contingent historical formulation; it follows that going back to the essence may involve an effort of interpretation and translation of historical data (for example, of the Mosaic Law and apocalyptic Messianism) and not simply its elimination. Christ came to bring a sword and fire, argues Sabatier, precisely in the sense that every expression of Christianity is also a constraint or an obstacle to be fought against; in this respect, we could speak of dialectical hermeneutics because each expression, however necessary, is in itself contradictory and has to be overcome. In the end the essence is precisely in this movement in which the spirit surpasses itself and breaks out of the forms in which it has been temporarily objectified: the essence is an act, never a state or a concept. "It is these contradictions and conflicts which set Christian thought in movement, and produced the life and progress of that early age, so that one may always rightly consider it as a creative and classic epoch, and hold it up as an example to the churches of all time; on condition, however, that it not be considered as an immutable mass of eternal verities, but taken in its natural movement, in its constant effort of progressive liberation from the past, in its heroic ascent towards religious forms and ideas, freer, more

---

[43] PR, pp. 179-80.

human, more conformed to the universal character, to the spirituality and to the pure morality of the religion of Jesus".[44]

Sabatier's conflict with Catholicism and his notion of Protestantism have deep philosophical roots in the German cultural tradition of the nineteenth century, especially in Idealism. He criticises the Catholic distinctions of natural and supernatural, morality and religion[45] because the principle of the incarnation is a principle of reconciliation, of synthesis. But this synthesis now realises itself in human life that has become free and responsible, in possession of itself; from this point of view there is no difference between the significance of the Reformation and the significance of the Enlightenment since both these movements combat the objectivism, the supernaturalism and extrinsicism of Catholicism. Initially the Reformers thought they could go back to primitive Christianity, but "history never recommences" and in this way Protestantism became one of the new and original forces of the modern world. "In Catholicism Christianity tends to realise itself as a theocratic institution; it becomes an external law, a supernatural power, which, from without, imposes itself on individuals and on peoples. In Protestantism, on the contrary, Christianity is brought back from the exterior to the interior; it plants itself in the soul as a principle of subjective inspiration which, acting organically on individual and social life, transforms it and elevates it progressively without denaturalising and doing violence to it. Protestant subjectivity becomes spontaneity and liberty, just as necessarily as Catholic objectivity becomes supernaturalism and clerical tyranny. The religious element is no longer separated from the moral element; it no longer asserts itself as a truth or morality superior to human truth and human morality... Man escapes from tutelage, and in all departments, comes into possession of himself, into the full and free development of his being, into his majority".[46] At this point therefore, Christianity is only a humanism and a morality (the coincidence of religion and morality) and the responsability for its meaning lies solely with the individual, or rather, with "modern" man who places his trust in values like progress, morality and science. A Christianity thus conceived is always "interior, invisible, ideal";[47] indeed, if we wanted to ironise a little with

---

[44] Cf. PR, pp. 181-92. On the complexity of the concept of "essence of Christianity" in Sabatier, cf. S. Sorrentino, "L'essenza del cristianesimo nella prospettiva di A.S.", *Filosofia e teologia* V (1991), pp. 45-57.

[45] PR, pp. 199-200.

[46] PR, pp. 204, 208-9.

[47] PR, p. 214.

Nietzsche we could say that it assumes "a form that is certainly of the purest and most transparent, but it is hardly visible"[48] since in point of fact it becomes philosophy; however, according to Sabatier, this is precisely the aim of the entire religious evolution which manifests itself ultimately in Protestantism. "By very reason of its superiority, and of the conditions of general culture that it presupposes, this form of Christianity could only appear after all the others. The spirit can only become self-conscious by distinguishing itself from the body in which at first it seems as if diffused, and by opposing to it an energetic moral protest... This new age of autonomy... could only commence in modern times — that is to say, with that general movement which, since the end of the Middle Ages, is leading humanity to an ever completer enfranchisement, and rendering it more universally and more individually responsible for its destinies". But this essence, which becomes manifest and clear in a definitive form only with modernity (and, it would appear, thanks to a sort of convergence or affinity with its fundamental values), is what was there also at the beginning, the Christianity of Jesus: "It may be remarked that by this evolution, and under its Protestant form, the Christian principle was only returning to its pure essence and its primitive expression. It could only recognise itself, take cognisance of its true nature... by remounting to its source, and by renewing its strength,through reflection and criticism, at its original springs. That is why Protestantism has taken the form of this return to the past, for in it Christianity does not surpass itself; it simply tries to know itself better and to become more faithful to its principle".[49]

---

[48] F. Nietzsche, *Vom Nutzen und Nachteil der Historie für das Leben, Sämtliche Werke*, Band II (Stuttgart: Alfred Kröner Verlag, 1964) pp. 154-55.

[49] PR, pp. 215-16.

II

Adolf Harnack's View of the "Essence of Christianity"

What is powerfully innovative in the debate about the "essence" of Christianity at the turn of the nineteenth century is the widespread endeavour to replace Greek philosophy with the modern scientific study of history as the cultural referent for the expounding of Christian truths. By comparing the Jewish element with the Greek element, beginning from the New Testament, attempts were made to eliminate the latter as later, superimposed or falsifying, and to use the former as frame of reference since by then the new philological and historical science (even leaving the mediation of the Church uncertain or undetermined) was able to apprehend it in its purity and independence from the other.

Even though Harnack's outlook is not very different from that of Sabatier, he would never have used the word "philosophy" in a title. He wished to be nothing more than an historian, but in the lectures he held at Berlin University in the winter of 1899-1900 his historical knowledge is without a doubt informed and upheld by a much wider vision, which is both philosophical and theological.[1] Troeltsch, (whose position we shall be

---

[1] Cf. A. Harnack, *Das Wesen des Christentums* (Leipzig: J.C. Hinrich Verlag, 1900; München & Hamburg: Siebenstern, 1964), to which page references of German edition refer. English translation by T.B. Saunders, *What is Christianity?* (New York: Putnam's Sons, 1901, 1904) indicated with the abbreviation WC. The first French translations of Harnack date back to 1893 (*Précis de l'histoire de dogmes* [Paris: Fischbacher]); *Das Wesen des Christentums* was translated into French almost immediately, in 1902 (and was completely revised in 1907), by the same publisher. The discussions about Harnack are affected in a decisive way by the writings of Loisy and Troeltsch whom we will be discussing, but also by others (cf. R. Anderson, *Rationalisme christianisé et haute critique, réponse à "l'Essence du Christianisme" du Prof. Harnack* [Paris: Fischbacher, 1905]; J. Rivière, *La propagation du christianisme dans les trois premiers siècles, d'après les conclusions de M. Harnack* [Paris: Bloud, 1907]).

discussing later on), considered it to be an idealistic and romantic philosophy of history because all the empirical material is interpreted according to a certain basic guiding idea, and it would not in any case be possible to find the essence on a purely historical plane, as Harnack believes he can do, but only on the basis of a particular faith or personal conviction.[2] In fact, however limited Harnack's philosophical or hermeneutical awareness might be, not even he places his whole trust simply in science: "What is Christianity? It is solely in its historical sense that we shall try to answer this question here; that is to say, we shall employ the methods of historical science and the experience of life gained by witnessing the actual course of history. We thus exclude the view of the question taken by the apologist and the religious philosopher". He states that he does not intend to concern himself with "the religious principle" (we might here remember the idealistic or positivist expositions that started out from a *concept* of religion, as Sabatier did) but only with Christianity, in an attempt to find out what it is; nevertheless, "the answer to this question may, we hope, also throw light by the way on the more comprehensive one, What is religion and what ought it to be to us?".[3] This is possible because the inquiry will bring to light an essence, a simple and universal meaning of the Gospel that coincides with the meaning of religion itself; this universality of the most profound religious nucleus cannot be identified in a purely objective sense, but only by starting out from the unity of human nature, from the fact that its needs or fundamental questions are substantially identical. "The Christian religion is something simple and sublime; it means *one* thing and one thing only: Eternal life in the midst of time, by the strength and under the eyes of God... Goethe once said: Mankind is always advancing and man always remains the same. It is to *man* that religion pertains — to man, as one who in the midst of all change and progress himself never

---

[2]　See the essay by E. Troeltsch, "Was heisst 'Wesen des Christentums'?", published in *Christliche Welt*, 1903, no. 17, and later in *Gesammelte Schriften*, Bd. II: *Zur religiösen Lage, Religionsphilosophie und Etik* (Tübingen: Mohr, 1913; Aalen: Scientia, 1962) pp. 386-451. Translations into English by the translator.

[3]　Cf. WC, p. 6. Important attempts to establish a general essence of religion developed a few years later in famous works that are not exactly philosophical like *Totem and Taboo* by S. Freud and *The Elementary Forms of the Religious Life* by E. Durkheim (both of 1912); but without doubt Harnack was already aiming at a clarification of the essence of religion through his historical research into Christianity. This intention was already explicit in the lecture given in Berlin in 1896, "Christentum und Geschichte", which was later published in *Reden und Aufsätze*, Bd. II (Giessen: Töpelmann, 1906) pp. 3-21.

changes". Harnack's presupposition is thus an unchanging anthropological basis, and, deriving from this, an essence of the Gospel and of religion in general, but at the same time he is wary of attributing such wide implications to his inquiry; he is suspicious and mistrustful of philosophy and, problematically, points to a possible unity in anthropology: "Had (these lectures) been delivered sixty years ago, it would have been our endeavour to arrive by speculative reasoning at some general conception of religion, and then to try to define the Christian religion accordingly. But we have rightly become scepticel about the value of this procedure. *Latet dolus in generalibus*. We know today that life cannot be spanned by general conceptions, and that there is no general conception of religion to which actual religions are related simply and solely as species to genus".[4]

Harnack's premisses appear to be not only methodological but in a certain sense also ontological. He considered "life" as a process of development that maintains the unity of the organism but enriches it constantly with new qualities, and he attributed these characteristics to Christianity precisely because he wanted to eliminate any possible doctrinal or intellectual fixity: "It is not a question of a 'doctrine' being handed down by uniform repetition or arbitrarily distorted; it is a question of a *life*, again and again kindled afresh, and now burning with a flame of its own... Just as we cannot obtain a complete knowledge of a tree without regarding not only its root and its stem but also its bark, its branches, and the way in which it blooms, so we cannot form any right estimate of the Christian religion unless we undertake a comprehensive inquiry that shall cover all the facts of its history".[5] Clearly, on the one hand it is important to avoid considering everything as relative and changing ("we must not be like the child who wanted to get at the kernel of a bulb, went on picking off the leaves until there was nothing left") but what would be most serious — and here it may be that Harnack is beginning to refer to Catholicism — would be a kind of sacralization which considers everything as equally necessary ("there is no such thing as either kernel or husk, growth or decay, but everything is of equal value and alike permanent"). On the contrary, many things have to be eliminated during the inquiry, which is clearly also a critique and a purification of the material handed down from the past; and this concerns the person of Christ Himself, if His humanity is

---

[4]   Cf. WC, pp. 8-9.
[5]   WC, p. 11. Cf. pp. 149-50. Saunders' translation "... unless we take our stand upon a comprehensive induction..." has been changed to "... unless we undertake a comprehensive inquiry...".

really to be taken seriously. It is not enough to give Him a human body and a human psyche; we have to think of Him what we generally think of all men. "To be a man means, in the first place, to possess a certain mental and spiritual disposition, determined in such and such a way, and thereby limited and circumscribed; and, in the second place, it means to be situated, with this interior disposition, in a historical environment which in its turn is also limited and circumscribed. Anything beyond this means to be not 'a man'".[6]

If these words were to be applied not only to the history of Christianity, but also to the historian who tries to understand it, we would have great difficulty in arriving at a universally valid essence. One could claim, as Troeltsch does, that the unity comes from the point of view or the personal conviction of the historian; one could, like Sabatier, end up with an individual pulverisation of the historical-philosophical perspective, which is in contrast with his attempt to establish the meaning of Christianity and of religious evolution. Harnack, however, does not mean to attribute to history a merely negative task of criticism with regard to every truth, but rather an affirmative task of reconstruction, which would fill the gap left by the great philosophical systems and would effectively counteract the relativistic and nihilistic tendencies that history, and science in general, have sown in European culture. "The historian, whose business and highest duty is to determine what is of permanent value, is of necessity required not to cleave to words, *but to find out what is essential...* There are only two possibilities here: either the Gospel is in all respects identical with its earliest form, in which case it came with its time, and with its time has departed; or else it contains something which, under differing historical forms, is of permanent validity". And, as we have seen with Sabatier, it is possible to interpret the relation between the essence or principle and its historical manifestations as a movement of revelation and progressive clarification having at least three essential phases: the initial phase, which is a model, at once an origin and a goal, then the Catholic phase and finally the Protestant one. For the moment Harnack does no more than confirm that identification and change are both necessary: "The history of the Church shows us in its very commencement that 'primitive Christianity' had to disappear in order that 'Christianity' might remain; and in the same way in later ages one metamorphosis followed upon another. From the beginning it was a question of getting rid of formulas, correcting

---

[6] WC, pp. 13-15.

expectations, altering ways of feeling, and this is a process to which there is no end. But by the very fact that our survey embraces the whole course as well as the inception, we enhance our standard of what is essential and of real value". But for Harnack, it is not recent developments that dominate the inquiry, as though it were a question of trying to construct a "modern" religion, one that is essentially new and original; on the contrary, what we gain from the evolution of Christianity (or from Protestantism) is a clarification or confirmation of what was there at the beginning, while the primitive form is the model of what we are searching for in the present and in the future. "We enhance our standard — but we need not wait to take it from the history of those later ages. The thing itself reveals it. We shall see that the Gospel in the Gospel is something so simple, something that speaks to us with so much power, that it cannot easily be mistaken... No one who possesses a fresh eye for what is alive, and true feeling for what is really great, can fail to see it and distinguish it from its contemporary guise".[7]

So, we have an essential nucleus, which means that we are no longer burdened by those historical and cultural roots that for Harnack constituted the humanity of the Saviour: "Jesus Christ's teaching will at once bring us by steps which, if few, will be large, to a height where its connexion with Judaism will appear only a loose one, and most of the threads leading from it into 'contemporary history' become of no importance at all". This nucleus can be grasped in relation to an anthropological element which, as I mentioned, can be considered in a circular way: as the condition for the understanding of the essence or as the result of the penetration of Christianity into humanity: "I entertain no doubt that even the founder had an eye to *man*, in whatever external situation he might be found — *man* who, at bottom, always remains the same, whether he be moving upwards or downwards, whether he be in riches or poverty, whether he be of strong mind or of weak".[8] If "in history absolute judgements are

---

[7]   WC, pp. 13-14. The "Gospel in the Gospel", the innermost and permanent nucleus, is the *moral* message of Christ, it is the Gospel "*of* Jesus", which is different, according to a distinction that is constantly recurrent in the book, from the Gospel "*about* Jesus", "that is about Christ who died and rose again", and was deified by early Christianity (note to p. 11 omitted in Saunders' translation. See p. 185 in German edition).

[8]   WC, pp. 16-18. In other words it could equally well be said that when the essential, permanent humanity that is in each one of us examines early historical data the result is an essential religion, an essential Christianity, and when Christianity delves right into the heart of man, then many things fall away and what remains of him is only what is eternally valid.

impossible" (these judgements are in any case "the creation of feeling and of will", a "subjective act" and not "the product of knowledge") it is because there exists no knowledge that in objective or positive terms can satisfy our every need ("all the needs of the mind and the heart"). If we were to trust exclusively in knowledge we would be prolonging the illusions of the nineteenth century in a wrong direction, in the direction of an untenable historiographical objectivism. Objectivity and truth have significance in relation to human life, but human life becomes unitary and comprehensible in the light of truth, thanks to the presence of God in history: "what a hopeless thing it would be for mankind if the higher peace to which it aspires, and the clearness, the certainty and the strength for which it strives, were dependent on the measure of its learning and its knowledge".[9]

It is clear how in this perspective the question of "demythologisation"[10] becomes central. When considering the concept of miracle, Harnack does not dismiss the problem in a 'miraculistic' evolutionism (which of its very nature makes the notion of miracle "pointless", as in Sabatier); rather, he argues in terms of an antithesis of kantian derivation between physics and ethics, necessity and freedom, and he stresses the psychic, interior significance of miracles. In ancient societies, he asserts, miracles were "of almost daily occurrence", also because "the strict conception which we now attach to the word 'miracle' was then unknown; it came in only with a knowledge of the laws of nature and their general validity". Nowadays we think that miracles in this sense, as "interruption of the order of nature", cannot exist; but we know that "the religious man... is certain that he is not shut up within a blind and brutal course of nature... This experience, which I might express in one word as the ability to escape from the power and the service of transitory things, is always felt afresh to be a miracle each time that it occurs". Thus a miracle represents an experience of liberation in mythical form; the conception of the divine "as a mighty power working upon the order of nature, and breaking through it" may well belong to the imagination or be metaphorical, but what counts is its interior significance: "It is not miracles that matter; the question on which everything turns is whether we are helplessly yoked to an inexorable necessity, or whether a God exists who rules and governs,

---

9   WC, p. 19.
10   I use this term, which is connected with the work of Bultmann, for a rapid indication of an issue which is present in Harnack, as it is in Sabatier, but which is not dealt with in any specific way. Cf. P. Boschini, *Escatologia senza storia. Storicismo e antistoricismo nel pensiero di R. Bultmann* (Bologna: Clueb, 1988).

and whose power, which is capable of compelling Nature, can be invoked and experienced".[11]

This opposition regarding the notion of miracle indicates a movement we have already seen towards the interiorisation or moralisation of belief, and therein consists the demythologisation as comprehension and translation; but this movement can also be interpreted as the historical maturation and positive evolution of religion, which will thus inevitably have its centre in evangelical Christianity, in the religion of Jesus Christ. In Harnack's view, already John the Baptist preannounced principally the "morality" and not a specific person ("the discriminating element, the only decisive reality is morality"), though it can be said that he preannounced Christ because the person of Christ coincides in substance with his moral message (the announcement *about* Jesus, about the incarnation, death and resurrection of God, does not seem to Harnack to be equally authentic or original). In fact, he argues, the concrete, physical or cosmological eschatology refers to the dependence of Jesus on the cultural conditions of his age while the spiritual or interior eschatology is his original message proper. Here too, as with miracles, Harnack wants to relate the mythical or imaginative manifestation to the moral truth (the preaching of the imminent end of the world points to the urgency of conversion, as the prophets and Christ himself proclaimed); or else he attributes the mythical (i.e. future and exterior) aspect of eschatology to the dimension of the "husk" and the moral (i.e. present and interior) aspect to the dimension of the "kernel".[12] Harnack here seems well aware that these distinctions between kernel and husk and between essence and manifestation are hardly feasible and pose an infinite number of questions. For example, we might ask: what exactly is the kernel, the substance of Harnack's interpretation of Christianity, and what are the historical incrustations that we can today ignore? And within this kernel or substance, what emerges as the substance of Christianity? What Harnack gives us is a selective criterion that revolves around the idea of something that is original, something new, which finds no explanation in the cultural conditions of the time, and he asks that this criterion be applied to himself too: "Let us hope that we may find fair judges, who will measure our ideas not by what we have unwittingly taken

---

[11]   Cf. WC, pp. 25-31 and pp. 153-54. Saunders' translation on p. 31 "... whose power to compel Nature we can move by prayer and make a part of our experience" has been changed to "... whose power, which is capable of compelling Nature, can be invoked and experienced".

[12]   WC, pp. 41-42, 55-57.

over from tradition and are neither able nor called upon to correct, but by what was born of our very own".[13]

What then, we can ask ourselves, does Harnack present that is really original and that does not "dissolve into the general ideas prevailing at the time"? Certainly not his claim to a pure and anti-philosophical scientific approach, nor his typically Protestant philosophy of history, and not even the demythologisation (transformation in terms of morality and psychology) of belief. Rather I would say that what is authentically new in Harnack is the connection between anthropology and theology, which we have hitherto dealt with too briefly. Christianity appears as the highest religion thanks to the moral and interior significance, the universally human significance, of its message. "But the fact that the whole of Jesus' message may be reduced to these two heads — God as the Father, and the human soul so ennobled that it can and does unite with Him — shows us that the Gospel is in no wise a positive religion like the rest; that it contains no statutory or particularistic elements; *that it is, therefore, religion itself*".[14] Also for Harnack, therefore, Christ is a historical-evolutionary factor in the creation of a higher religiosity since "he took a vigorous hold of all fumbling and stammering attempts at religion and brought them to their issue": to represent Christianity "as an ethical message is no depreciation of its value" and its theme is "ordinary morality", which had also been the purpose of John the Baptist's preaching. "It was in this sense that Jesus combined religion and morality, and in this sense religion may be called the soul of morality and morality the body of religion. We can thus understand how it was that Jesus could place the love of God and the love of one's neighbour side by side and consider them identical; the love of one's neighbour is the only practical proof on earth of that love of God which finds its life in humility".[15]

But if the moral or human aspect is the revelation "on earth" of what is true and essential in religion, then religion knows what is true and essential in man of any age and tries constantly to lead him back to this secret, interior nucleus from the variety of human conditions and activities. "The Gospel makes its appeal to the inner man, who, whether he is healthy or sick, in a happy position or a miserable one... always remains the same... What the Gospel says is this: whoever you may be, and whatever your

---

[13]   WC, p. 56.
[14]   WC, p. 65.
[15]   WC, pp. 72-75. Cf. also pp. 41, 42-44.

position... your real business in life is always the same. There is only *one* relation and *one* idea which you must not violate, and in the face of which all others are only varied trappings and vain show: to be a child of God and a citizen of His kingdom, and to exercise love". In this sense it seems to me that the originality of Harnack can be identified in this circularity, which means that religion tells us the truth about man, and man the truth about religion. In fact, precisely because "the forces of the Gospel appeal to the deepest foundations of human existence... if a man is unable to go down to the root of humanity, and has no feeling for it and no knowledge of it, he will fail to understand the Gospel.[16]

As we have said, Harnack distinguishes between the "Gospel of Jesus" and the "Gospel about Jesus", in a characteristically anti-Catholic way that has far-reaching hermeneutical implications. The situation is made more complex by the fact that, separately or together, various criteria for the selection and interpretation of material are applied, and the aim is to decide what is original and authentic in Christianity and what is not. First of all, there is the criterion of psychological reduction that we have already seen at work in the attempt to define the significance of miracles and of the "exterior" doctrine of the Revelation of Judaic derivation (as well as in the work of Sabatier, where reference to the more general human experience of responsibility and guilt made possible the elimination of the biblical account of the Fall). For example, we cannot say anything of the filial union of Jesus with God (which was felt and proclaimed to be unique) because we cannot experience within ouselves anything similar to it: "Only a man who had had a similar experience himself could do anything to fathom this mystery. Let a prophet try to raise the veil, but, for our part, we must be content with the fact that this Jesus who preached humility and knowledge of self nevertheless named himself and himself alone as *the Son of God*".[17] But the concept of the Messiah is different; although it was Jesus who took it over from the Jewish tradition and made it "explode" by endowing it with a new content, we can find in ourselves a corresponding experience, in the interest that we have in the prospect of the social renewal and moral evolution of humanity: "we can still feel some of its meaning... In the prospect of a Messianic period we see once more the old hope of a golden age; the hope which, when moralised, must necessarily be the goal

---

[16]   WC, pp. 118, 127, 132. Cf. A. Sabatier, PR, p. 158: "He was content to place himself at the centre of the human consciousness and to dig down to the source of life. He takes man as he is in all climates and in all conditions".

[17]   WC, p. 132.

of every vigorous movement in human life and forms an inalienable element in the religious view of history".[18] Also the idea of a sacrificial death, the idea "that by his death in suffering he did a definitive work; and that he did it 'for us'" is something that has to be felt rather than established doctrinally: "Were we to attempt to measure and register this decisive fact, as was soon attempted, we should fall into dreadful paradoxes; but we can in our turn feel it for ourselves with the same freedom with which it was originally felt".[19]

There are then other criteria of interpretation, historical and philological criteria, which have as premiss and issue the idea that underlies the whole book, namely that Jesus, *as God*, is not the content of the Christian message ("In those leading features of it which we described in the earlier lectures the whole of the Gospel is contained, and we must keep it free from the intrusion of any alien element: God and the soul, the soul and its God... *The Gospel, as Jesus proclaimed it, has to do with the Father only and not with the Son*"). Harnack adds immediately that he is well aware that the content of the writings of the Evangelists, and of St. Paul, is in fact Christ, but this is a later, Catholic transformation of the original nucleus and this is indicated by the words "as Jesus proclaimed it".[20] There thus emerges an opposition between original and derived, authentic and spurious, which Harnack makes use of to eliminate the Catholic arguments about the divine and cosmic nature of Christ; expressions that are particularly unfavourable to his basic thesis are interpreted in various ways and are attributed to the sphere of what is derived and inauthentic. "No man knoweth the Son but the Father; neither knoweth any man the Father, save the Son, and he to whomsoever the Son will reveal him": here Harnack makes Sonship dependent on our knowledge of God, in the sense that to recognise God as Father, as our Father, is to be His son. In this way the quality of son is given a metaphorical and not a realistic nature: to say one is a son of God is a way of declaring one knows God ("It is *knowledge of God* that makes the sphere of the divine Sonship... Rightly understood, the name of Son means nothing but the knowledge of God"), but this does not explain the first part of the statement, which confers an exceptional importance on the figure of Christ ("No man knoweth the Son but the Father"); Harnack

---

[18]   WC, pp. 144-45.
[19]   WC, p. 163.
[20]   Cf. WC, pp. 146-47 and note to p. 147, omitted in Saunders' translation (see p. 188, note to p. 92, in German edition).

was later to declare this "not original". "Thou lovedst me before the foundation of the world": after an attempt at psychology ("The confidence with which John makes him address the Father... is undoubtedly the direct reflection of the certainty with which Jesus himself spoke"), the negative light of criticism falls on this sentence because "its authenticity cannot be supported". "The Father hath committed all things unto me": Harnack argues that this "cannot possibly really mean 'all things' but rather 'everything', that is to say, 'all knowledge', i.e. the whole doctrine".[21] Similarly it is claimed that if the oldest tradition admitted that the Messianic consciousness of Jesus was founded "not on his baptism by John the Baptist but on the transfiguration" then "the account of a special Messianic experience which Jesus had at his baptism certainly belongs to a very old tradition but not to the original tradition and therefore it must be considered a legend"; or, regarding the temptations in the wilderness, that "if the story of the vision at his baptism is not original, then also the story of the temptations must be apocryphal or it must belong to a later period".[22]

What I want to show with these examples is that what Harnack considers *original* is also rational and true (in the sense of a psychological or ethical reduction, what we too can experience: the essence of Christianity) and what he considers *derived* or subsequent is imaginary, legendary, mythical, it is the non-truth and that which cannot be experienced, which came later (viz. Catholicism) and of which we must free ourselves. And that is not all: we cannot take as "original" anything prior to the testimony of the early Church, or in other words, as Harnack puts it: "the original tradition is not for all this a pure tradition as it has already had contact with the convictions and judgements of faith". Is all this not sufficient to make Harnack's whole approach problematical, given that the Gospel *about* Jesus is the message of the primitive Christian community, that Jesus "constitutes the true content" of the Gospel "in the form in which St. Paul and the Evangelists proclaimed it"?[23]

Harnack's reference to Schleiermacher's idea of a religion that is experienced leads to a simplification of the religious question and, sometimes, paradoxically, to its transformation into philosophy. Harnack

---

21 Cf. WC, pp. 130-32 and note to p. 132, omitted in Saunders' translation (see p.187, note to p. 85, in German edition).

22 WC, note to p. 143, omitted in Saunders' translation (see p. 187, note to p. 89, in German edition).

23 Cf. WC, note to p. 23; note to p. 147; both omitted in Saunders' translation (see p. 185, note to p. 26, and p. 188, note to p. 92, in German edition).

is so convinced that any doctrine is purely human and historical ("The Gospel is not a theoretical doctrine, it is not earthly wisdom"), that he risks reducing Christianity to a formula, to something rational ("God and the soul, the soul and its God"). Or, by avoiding the problem of a redeemed human reason, he risks falling into a vitalism without principles according to which "it is only the religion which a man has himself experienced that is to be confessed... If there is no broad 'doctrine of religion' to be found in the Gospel, still less is there any direction that a man is to begin by accepting and confessing any ready-made doctrine".[24] However, we know that there exists an objective and immutable nucleus of Christian truths, but this becomes evident to us only through a demythologisation that shows the connection between what is permanent in man and what is permanent in the Gospel: "The Gospel, it is said,... is indissolubly connected with an antiquated view of the world and history... No doubt it is true that the view of the world and history with which the Gospel is connected is quite different from ours, and that view we cannot recall to life, and would not if we could; but 'indissoluble' the connexion is not. I have tried to show what the essential elements in the Gospel are, and these elements are 'timeless'. Not only are they so; but the man to whom the Gospel addresses itself is also 'timeless', that is, it addresses itself to *man*, who, in spite of all progress and development, never changes in his inmost constitution and in his fundamental relations with the external world".[25] But immediately afterwards, the essential content of the Gospel, which this demythologisation has laboriously saved from the changing and perishing of all things, is presented in terms of a philosophical and ethical *dualism* that Harnack has clearly borrowed from nineteenth century Kantism. "The Gospel is based — and this is the all important element in the view which it takes of the world and history — upon the antithesis between Spirit and flesh, God and the world, good and evil... In the end, then, it is essentially a matter of indifference what name we give to the opposition with which every man of ethical feeling is concerned: God and the world, the Here and the beyond, the visible and the invisible, matter and spirit, the life of impulse and the life of freedom, physics and ethics". With this Harnack re-proposes the basic approach that we found underlying his psychological or ethical interpretation of miracle (the liberation from necessity) and he even attempts to go beyond the opposition mentioned in the sphere of

---

[24]   Cf. WC, p. 151. Saunders' translation of *Religionslehre* as "theory" in this passage has been changed to "doctrine".

[25]   WC, p. 152.

morality by using the neo-kantian concept of "infinite task": "it is only by a struggle that this unity can be attained and it takes the form of an infinite task that can be accomplished only tendentially", even if "we are unable to bring our knowledge in space and time, together with the contents of our inner life, into the unity of a global vision of the world". Nevertheless, the "truth" of this struggle, of the surpassing of material or purely instinctive necessity "holds good for all time, and it forms the essential element in the dramatic pictures of contemporary life in which the Gospel, fruit of its age, expresses the antithesis that is to be overcome".[26] The decisive conflict between matter and spirit, evil and good etc. "forms the essential element" of the Gospel (which otherwise remains immersed in the mythological relativity of another time and another vision of the world); and together with this it obviously forms the essential element of man, for what is more universally and profoundly human than this rebellion against the power of matter and of instinct? The real miracle, the "decisive question" is whether we want to seek freedom *from* the world, or whether we succumb to the world, to its rules and to its spirit. In this way it is only in the sphere of *morality* that the essence of religion and the essence of man coincide.

In the second half of these lectures Harnack describes "the history of Christian religion in its leading phases",[27] but he cannot do this without making explicit his Protestant philosophy of history, which had already been evident at various points. If we take as the connecting theme the distinction between kernel and husk which here too has a very important role, we can note that: 1) The appearance of the kernel or essence is not primarily the result of historical research but of the evolution of Christian life. Even at the beginning "what was kernel and what was husk, history has itself showed with unmistakable plainness, and by the shortest process. Husk were the whole of the Jewish limitations attaching to Jesus' message...

---

[26] WC, pp. 153-154. Saunders' translation on p. 153 "... and when it is attained it takes the form of a problem that is infinite and only approximately soluble" has been changed to "... and it takes the form of an infinite task that can be accomplished only tendentially". Also, on p. 154, "... the unity of a philosophic theory of the world" has been changed to "... the unity of a global vision of the world".

[27] WC, p. 155. Cf. also A. Harnack, "Die evangelisch-soziale Aufgabe im Lichte der Geschichte der Kirche" (lecture delivered on May 17, 1894 at the Social-Evangelical Congress in Frankfurt a. M.), and the already mentioned Berlin lecture of 1896, "Christentum und Geschichte", in *Reden und Aufsätze*, Bd.II, pp. 3-76.

Without doing violence to the inner and essential features of the Gospel... Paul transformed it into the universal religion".[28] This means that historical research is part of a wider vital process, it is at the service of this process and at the same time it finds its justification in it. 2) On the other hand this process of purification has no end because one historical "coating" of the essence is followed by another. In this sense Harnack has perhaps not developed his hermeneutics sufficiently: he sees each historical manifestation as a barrier, a limit, an alteration that means that access to the kernel is made more difficult, and at the same time as the necessary translation of the essence into the language of a certain civilisation or historical context. "But whilst the original limitations fell away, new ones of necessity made their appearance; and they modified the simplicity and the power of a movement which was from within".[29] 3) The Gospel is a life, not a doctrine, and therefore it is not adequately expressed in any of its juridical, political or philosophical "husks"; but all these husks keep it alive and re-propose its basic content to humanity again and again: "The Gospel did not come into the world as a statutory religion and therefore none of the forms in which it assumed intellectual and social expression — not even the earliest — can be regarded as possessing a classical and permanent character... As a Gospel it (the Christian religion) has only *one* aim - the finding of the living God, the finding of Him by every individual as *his* God, and as the source of strength and joy and peace. How this aim is progressively realised through the centuries... or whatever other kinds of bark there may be which protect the core and allow the sap to rise, is a matter that is secondary, that is exposed to change, that belongs to the centuries, that comes with them and with them perishes".[30] 4) Alongside this positive conception of the manifestation or "husk" (given that we have the essence only in that, and "anything beyond this means to be not 'a man'"), there is the negative conception that sees the outer coating as decadence, probably a borrowing from Overbeck who had distinguished between a primitive Christianity and a historical Christianity. "To be sure, a husk and outer coating had already formed around this religion, it had become more difficult to penetrate them and to reach the kernel, and it had also lost something of its original life".[31] 5) But this too is only one side

---

[28]   WC, p. 183.

[29]   *Ibid.*

[30]   WC, pp. 193-94.

[31]   WC, p. 220. According to Overbeck, Christianity aimed at a life beyond the world, and awaited the imminent end and the return of Christ; but since this

of the problem because, within this context of a negative conception of the husk, Christianity, oppressed by its own manifestations, tends to free itself of them and to show increasingly clearly through history what it really is. It was Protestantism in particular that set this process in motion after Greek and Roman Catholicism, but in the work of Luther the *principles* of the Reformation were realised in a distorted and regressive way ("there were countless problems of which he did not even know, to say nothing of being able to solve them; and so it was that he had no means of distinguishing between kernel and husk, between what was original and what was of alien growth", and so "future development" is still to be reckoned with).[32]
6) All this makes the role of the historian in the modern evolution of Christianity much clearer - it is not an exclusively scientific role, it is also ecclesial and spiritual. If we look for "the essence and kernel of our religion" and see our (personal and denominational) religious position "as *one* branch of a huge tree", writes Harnack in a preface of 1903, it is in order to provide a solid basis for dialogue and unification; and this movement from the "husk", from the particular historical element, towards the universal "kernel" is the *meaning* of Christian development and also of the work of the historian. "No historian who really reflects could ever be convinced that this is not a historical, and opportune, task. Historical understanding begins only when there is the endeavour to free the essential and specific element of a great phenomenon from its contemporary historical wrapping".[33] Again many years later, in 1925, Harnack defined the task of the historian with almost the same words, reaffirming that personal involvement and in general what in the first lecture he had called "the experience of life gained by witnessing the actual course of history" cannot justify arbitrary or unilateral approaches which would render futile that

---

expectation was disappointed and it came to be *in* the world, becoming involved in it and its various civilisations, now Christianity, like other great *historical* events, has nothing before it but a "decorous end" (cf. K. Löwith, *Von Hegel zu Nietsche* [Stuttgart: W. Kohlhammer, 1958] pp. 402-415). Overbeck's position was at least in part based on that of the early Nietzsche (his colleague in Basle), who held that authentic Greek tragedy is a sublime and unrepeatable moment that is immediately lost through rationalisation, the Socratic science. And Nietzsche was convinced that this schema could be applied to Christianity, in the sense that a "modern" Christianity, mainly learned or scientific, was contradictory and destined to failure. Harnack's book is also a reply to this position and to that of Overbeck (cf. G. Forni, *Sullo storicismo. Appunti per la relazione Nietzsche-Barth*, in *Studi di ermeneutica*, cit., pp. 153-59).

[32] WC, pp. 295-97.
[33] Omitted in English translation. In German edition p. 181 (Vier Vorreden n. 2).

task of unification that the historian explicitly takes upon himself: "*It is a task of history to determine the essence of Christianity* because this religion contains a message that was brought to fulfilment in history. Only he who has become part of it can do it justice, but if he puts his experiences in the place of objective reality, or if he takes from this reality only parts and makes them the foundation for the whole, or if he allows the particular religion to merge into some general mysticism, then how is it possible to reach the essence of Christianity and make it universally recognised?".[34] So, along the path of authentic Christianity both progressions and regressions are possible; and every major turning-point is marked by the action and the sacrifice of a small number of men. Speaking of the notion of "Messiah", he had already said that "it is *persons* who form the saving element in history", and now he repeats it when talking of the sacrifice of Christ: "the sufferings of the pure and the just are the saving element (in history)".[35] This confirms the historical-evolutionary function of sacrifice ("it is not words, but deeds, and not deeds only but self-sacrificing deeds... that form the turning-point in every great advance in history"); the early Christians were aware that "on them the progress of history rested" and that "the last and highest stage in the history of humanity had been reached".[36] However, even if this is essentially true, a long series of events, both positive and negative, had still to manifest themselves: in fact, as a moral proclamation, founded in the freedom and interiority of the relation between man and God, and as universal inner life, Christianity is progression; but it is regression in that it is bound to particular institutions, laws or customs, or to particular dogmatic, metaphysical and mythological developments; it is progression as Protestantism (which is "kernel", "essence"), it is regression as Catholicism (which is "husk"); it is progression as the Gospel *of* Jesus, it is regression as the Gospel *about* Jesus. With regard to this, further clarifications are given[37] and, for example, it is said of the work of St. Paul: "it is a perverse proceeding to make Christology the fundamental substance of the Gospel", in the sense that, from being a moral message, the Gospel is deformed in a metaphysical-theological sense, with speculations about "the entrance of a divine being into the world". This is one of the most serious "alterations"; there are others regarding the evolution of the Church, which initially is "something suprasensible and

---

[34] Omitted in English translation. In German edition p. 183 (Vier Vorreden n. 4).
[35] WC, pp. 145, 161.
[36] WC, pp. 161, 192.
[37] WC, pp. 187-89.

heavenly, because it came from within" and subsequently it receives a "body" in constant growth, an "exterior dimension". Harnack asserts both the "necessity" for Christianity to set up a new community to oppose the Jewish community, and the corruption or falsification that in this way creeps into the original message.[38]

What emerges then is a certain criticism of Greek and Roman Catholicism, the main points of which can now be identified quite clearly. The cosmic-metaphysical developments of Christology, centred around the Greek notion of Logos, appear to Harnack "inadmissible": they have destroyed "the simplicity of the Gospel, and increasingly transformed it into a philosophy of religion", though he admits that, "for that age", they had a positive validity for Christian preaching in the Greek and Roman worlds.[39] The theory of the human-divine nature of Christ is "alien" to the Gospel, "the whole fabric of *ecclesiastical* Christology is a thing absolutely outside the *concrete personality* of Jesus Christ".[40] Naturally the Greek Church — and later also the Roman Church — represents a regression, a return to classical and pagan antiquity, because it made Christianity, which was a "life", into a "doctrine",[41] putting the moral and interior element on one side and developing the external ritualistic aspects of worship.[42] Instead Protestantism is a "return to the origins" and so for it the search for the essence or kernel, if taken to mean the "Gospel of Jesus" and not "primiti-

---

[38]   WC, pp. 183-86. Cf. p. 191: "Our purest and most sacred possessions, when they leave the inward realm and pass into the world of form and circumstance, are no exception to the rule that the very shape which they take in action also proves to be their limitation".

[39]   WC, pp. 205-8.

[40]   WC, pp. 232-38.

[41]   WC, pp. 214-15, 228-30.

[42]   WC, pp. 240-48, 268-71. It is on these pages that Harnack presents the famous thesis of the "Hellenisation of Christianity": Greek Catholicism of the first centuries *takes the form, not of a Christian product in Greek dress, but of a Greek product in Christian dress* (p. 224). Cf. E.P. Meyering, *Die Hellenisierung des Christentums im Urteil Adolf von Harnacks* (Amsterdam: North-Holland Publ., 1985). More recent history of dogma has variously criticised Harnack's thesis. The position of the Catholic theologian A. Grillmeier is significant: several times between 1951 and 1979 he put forward the thesis that "the two heretical forms of Logos-sarx Christology, the Arian heresy and the Apollinarian heresy, are probably the most serious and dangerous encroachments by Hellenistic ideas upon the traditional conception of Christ"; viceversa, in the Chalcedonian Christological dogma there begins "a slow inverse process of de-Hellenisation that continues throughout the following centuries". Cf. *Jesus der Christus im Glauben der Kirche*, 1.1 (Freiburg-Basel-Wien: Herder, 1979).

III

Troeltsch: Observations on Harnack's Method

The position held by Ernst Troeltsch, which is close to that of Harnack and Sabatier, is clearly expounded in his work written in 1902, *The Absoluteness of Christianity and the History of Religions.*[1] His basic intention of reconciling Christianity and the modern world constitutes a "critical reduction" with regard to the body of traditions inherited, and a progressive vision of history and of religious evolution, in the sense of an ever-increasing spiritualisation or interiorisation of beliefs. Troeltsch was tendentially anti-Catholic and anti-Scholastic and he believed that an adequate distinction of the areas of influence (real-ideal, nature-spirit, exterior-interior) would eliminate all conflicts between faith and science, between the Christian spirit and modern civilisation; moreover, his refusal to attribute to faith any concrete knowledge of reality (either natural or historical) freed him of dated visions of the world and of metaphysical representations that were by that time unacceptable. It is therefore necessary to reformulate the concepts of providence, faith and miracle so as to remove them from Catholic extrinsicism and bring them back exclusively to the interior sphere. In this sense religious faith has nothing to do with a scientific explanation of facts: it does not want to replace science (because our faith does not tell us how God operates in the world) but it cannot be disputed either (because science cannot deny that the world is nonetheless governed by God). In the same way, if we speak of "truth" as the content of the Christian message, it can in no way be a truth that interferes with philosophical or scientific research: in the case of religion it is not a theoretical but a practical truth, an aspiration towards the supreme good that makes use of cognitive elements but is not formally knowledge. We can see that we here find ourselves close to the neo-kantian distinction between physics

---

[1]   The English translation used is by David Reid (London: SCM Press, 1972) (identified as AC), already mentioned in chapter I, note 17.

and ethics (external-internal, nature-spirit), that had been of interest to Harnack; but what is more important is that this approach demonstrates one of the possible meanings of the late-Protestant insistence on Christianity as "life" and "experience": Christianity is not science, it is not a matter of knowing about a truth in a theoretical sense. Even the distinction between "Church" and "community" expresses the interiorisation of religion, because the "community" is invisible, purely spiritual, whereas the "Church" is disregarded because it is an institution founded on miracles, sacramentalism and authority. This interiorisation (to which corresponds the secularisation or laicisation of the world) also marks the basic direction of Troeltsch's philosophy of history.[2]

The opposition between "inner miracle" (which Troeltsch rightly says is indemonstrable) and "exterior miracle", which is comprehensible in the theoretical situation we have outlined (the insistence on the former is clearly a reaction to the rationalistic-metaphysical objectivism of the latter), could be criticised on various accounts.[3] The inner miracle is conversion, which enables us to see the exterior miracle; the exterior miracle is the occasion for a conversion, the faith of the Church produces conversions (the relationship between community and individual) and in as much as it is the faith of a community, produced and sustained by God, it comprehends and defines the action of God in the world. It is not clear what exactly is "inner" and what "exterior". Nevertheless, by combatting Catholic supernaturalism and interiorising the notion of miracle, the Protestant and modernist tendencies make the history of the Church and the history of the world coincide (and therefore the "interiority" necessarily becomes only

---

[2]   This division is in line with the "modernisation" of Christianity because it tends to make it compatible with the world of science and technology, with the "rationalisation" that has spread to every aspect of life. But a purely interior Christianity is in reality evanescent and on the verge of disappearing, as Nietzsche and Weber had already understood; it is not therefore a question of leaving the external physical world to scientific rationality, or material goods to market forces, and retaining the all-too-easily conquered citadel of inner life for miracles and divine action. The problem has been dealt with in an interesting way by Lukács, when he speaks of the practical philosophy of Kant: "At the end of the *Critique of Practical Reason*, the 'eternal, bronzen' legality of natural happenings and the purely interior freedom of individual ethical praxis appear as incompatibly separate bases of human existence, but which at the same time are irremovably given in their separation" (G. Lukács, *Geschichte und Klassenbewusstsein*, vol. 2 [Neuwied & Berlin: Luchterhand, 1968] p. 314). Translator's translation.

[3]   Cf. AC, pp. 51-52, 59-60.

individual). But if the world, as a single unit, is put into the hands of science, which considers it in its godless worldliness as an interweaving of causal relations that on principle are sufficient to determine the meaning of every event, it is difficult to see either how a historiography of the Church is possible (I mean, a historiography in which the Church, in the fullness of its theological attributes, is the subject as well as the object of investigation) or how an authentically historical understanding of the events of salvation, like the Incarnation or the Resurrection, is possible. The consideration of every event as an event within the world, which is a fundamental methodological principle of modern science, finds confirmation in the late-Protestant division between internal and external, and there is only one possible conclusion to this: to deny that the events of salvation are "historical facts", which was what was happening at that time in the work of Alfred Loisy.[4]

Troeltsch too argues for a philosophy of history: the early stages of civilisation are "low", characterised by a dispersive multiplicity, exteriority and monotonous repetition ("nature"), while the "high" stages are characterised by interiority, creativity-innovation and unification ("spirit"). The higher religions, and in particular Christianity, have a historical-teleological role in the opposition to "the merely natural world" and in the development of a spiritual world, but this does not come about exclusively, or even principally, in Christianity.[5] A philosophy of history is not contemplated in the external-internal distinction we have outlined; on the

---

[4] An important, and difficult, question is to understand what is meant here by "history". It is not purely and simply history as a "science", because like other sciences (sociology, psychology) in the second half of the 19th century it was based on theoretical premises taken from the field of philosophy and even theology. In general it is a historical science sustained by an explicit or implicit philosophy of history; its decisive values seem in this sense to be (subordinate or superordinate to Christianity?) scientific "truth" and the "progress" of humanity. However, if it is not already a science, history wants increasingly to become one, abandoning philosophy as much as possible and assuming the methical criteria of the established sciences. It operates on the supposition that the world, as universal causal connection, is the the theatre, enclosed in on itself, of every possible event; on this basis, to speak of "historical event" is to speak of a causally determined event that is wholly part of the universal connection (in part unknown, but in itself determined) that is the world. When this science is applied to Christianity the outcome will be first of all that the fundamental moments of the intervention of God in history cannot be considered "historical events", precisely because they put the world in contact with what is both prior to and beyond it.

[5] AC, pp. 92-93.

contrary it would seem to be in contrast with it because it tends towards a synthesis of moral or religious values and empirical facts. But Troeltsch asserts that a philosophy of history is necessary: it is important, he says, to conserve "the religious belief in the unity and meaningfulness of reality", and possibly also to maintain "the metaphysical idea of a transcendent background of history", so as to avoid the possible relativistic or nihilistic results of historical research left to its own devices. And the process of unification will continue until there is a "victory of the highest values" and "the incorporation of all reality into their frame of reference"; in this way, in Troeltsch's view, also the concept of evolution is justified and without doubt he knows and thinks highly of Bergson's evolutionism.[6] But this point of view is later relativised when he refers to the individual and collective "concrete situation", to the "personal and, in the last analysis, subjective conviction" that is implicit in any vision of this kind, and to "practical, subjective valuations and attitudes".[7] If all this were true, we could interpret this philosophy of history as the expression of a personal conception of values which is confessional, and fundamentally religious (it is religion that, with an ethical motivation behind it, seeks the ways of salvation); and in fact a number of typical statements Troeltsch makes seem to be leading in this direction.[8] However, subsequently, this very philosophy of history is presented as a scientific vision of religion, as the result of a conforming to a modern scientific outlook; and this raises the question of the intentionally synthetic nature of this philosophy, which has no intention of committing itself unilaterally either to the dimension of science or to that of faith.[9]

Troeltsch has an essentially moral understanding of religion: he does not believe that a concept of religion is realised progressively in the course of history and finds its highest expression in Christianity, though he is nearer to this position than he himself thinks. For him there is a "personalistic understanding of redemption" that will never end even if the Christianity we know (bound to the person of Jesus) will come to an end and others will

---

[6]   AC, pp. 94, 100-101. The mention of the "extremely interesting works" by Henri Bergson is on p. 170.

[7]   Cf. AC, pp. 96, 102, 105.

[8]   Cf. AC, p. 107 ("a matter of personal conviction") and p. 112 ("purely a matter of religious conviction").

[9]   Cf. AC, pp. 131 ff. Cf. P. Boschini, "Storia e metafisica. Presupposti filosofici della teologia come scienza storica in E. Troeltsch (1898-1903)", *Filosofia e teologia* V (1991), pp. 40-44.

take its place.[10] He does not, however, deny that there is present in Christianity "an authentic revelation of God" (though he certainly does deny — also on the basis of the historicist premises noted above — that Christ is the definitive revelation of God, the Incarnation and the Resurrection); on the contrary, every great religion manifests a variety of revelations of God until we arrive at the revelation of "personalistic religion" embodied in Christianity, which, relatively speaking, is the most recent ("in our cultural context and in our moment of history").[11] Clearly a position of this kind could also be non-Christian ("With this way of thinking do we still find ourselves within the bounds of Christianity?"[12]), but merely philosophical, because in the end what remains is always only a certain concept of religion and not necessarily the historical religion that is a particular "embodiment"[13] of that concept. This is a problem that, as we have seen, affects the whole of Protestant thought of this period (also because the appeals to interiorisation and spiritualisation seem to owe much to the idealistic notion of "spirit") and that Nietzsche had already sensed in the sarcastic comments in his *Unzeitgemässe Betrachtungen*, II (1874).

The overall significance of Troeltsch's contribution to the debate is to bring to philosophical consciousness what in Harnack seems to be simply the result of a historiographical operation: to establish an essence of Christianity is at once a historical and philosophical-religious task because it entails clarification of the intellectual condition of modern man, of the importance that the historical and philological sciences assume for him and of the significance of the personal, existential choices that orientate the inquiry.[14] Troeltsch evidently believes that in Harnack a privileged relation

---

[10]   AC, pp. 115-16. Cf. F.W. Graf, "Max Weber e la teologia protestante del suo tempo", in *Max Weber e le scienze sociali del suo tempo*, edited by M. Losito and P. Schiera (Bologna: Il Mulino, 1988) pp. 312-17: in Troeltsch, "religion provides a central energy for the individual thanks to its ethical substance"; this makes it at once "a relativizing factor of political domination" and a factor of "social integration" by virtue of its "communicative potentialities".

[11]   AC, pp. 103, 122-23, 128-29.

[12]   AC, p. 131.

[13]   AC, p. 116.

[14]   Cf. the essay "Was heisst 'Wesen des Christentums'?" of 1903, already cited in chapter II, note 2 (abbreviation WH). Here Troeltsch develops the implications of his historical-religious method, previously dealt with in an important article of 1900, "Über die historische und dogmatische Methode in der Theologie" (Tübingen: 1900) (later reprinted in Ernst Troeltsch, *Gesammelte Schriften*, Band 2 [Tübingen: Mohr, 1913; Aalen: Scientia, 1962] pp.729-753). Quotations translated by translator.

between "essence" and primitive Christianity can be identified and in this he recalls the position of some critics, according to whom "the 'essence' is to be found in an 'idea' distinct from the individual manifestations, and also from the primitive form, and is expressed solely in all the forms and manifestations as a whole. These critics interpret the relation of primitive Christianity and the message of Jesus with the later development of Christianity in a different way from Harnack and see a looser connection between the concept of 'essence' and the primitive historical form".[15] However, as we have seen, the whole question of the humanity of Jesus (the inevitable partiality and limits of his perspective, because conditioned by Jewish culture) goes in the opposite direction and only one particular convergence can be identified between the "essence" and the "Gospel of Jesus", if by this latter expression we mean the most original nucleus of the primitive teaching that has been previously demythologised (purified of its Jewish wrapping). If by "primitive Christianity" we should mean the Gospel *about* Jesus preached by the first communities, by the Evangelists and by St.Paul, then we know that in Harnack's view we do not find the essence of the Gospel, but rather a corruption or falsification of it.

But whatever the outcome of this particular problem,[16] it is clear that Troeltsch does not think of Harnack's notion of "essence" as one concrete historical situation ("primitive Christianity") that becomes a measuring stick for others, but rather as a criterion or concept, arrived at through abstraction, that judges every historical situation. If this is true, it has to be recognised, however, that empirical historiography is not able to find such a criterion without making reference to some general presuppositions of a philosophy of history. The concept of essence "involves the application of a methodological principle and of a widely-experimented presupposition of modern historiography in general: vast interconnected systems of historical phenomena are the development of an idea, of a value, of a series of thoughts... The "essence" of such a system is the abstract concept, *the specific abstraction of history*, by dint of which the whole sphere of the interconnected formations, known and studied in detail, is understood from the fundamental guiding principle and its development".[17] What characterises Harnack's undertaking as a particular way of looking at the problem is precisely the privilege granted to the historical method and its philosophical premises, which Troeltsch shares but at the same time interprets as the

---

[15]   WH, p. 388.
[16]   Which is nevertheless dealt with again later: cf. WH, pp. 413-14, 422-23.
[17]   WH, p. 393.

specific culture of modernity. For this method, "miracles cease to be a means of discerning and determining the essence", but on the contrary "the determination of the essence is independent of the canon of the Bible, of miracles, of the Church and of dogma and points to the principle that reveals itself in its totality".[18]

However, the method must be bound to certain philosophical premises, in particular idealistic ones, because "in order to proceed historically, the abstraction ascertaining the essence of Christianity in any case needs the comparative history of religions and also, of late, the highest abstractions of the history of culture in general. In fact, it can ascertain the essence of Christianity only in as much as it conceives of Christianity as part of an overall religious and cultural development, within which every peculiarity of a particular sphere, every specific essence, is simply a form of the general life of the spirit and of its evolution".[19] In this way, Troeltsch is in complete agreement with Harnack if it is a question of asserting the end of Catholic supernaturalism and a decisive change to a historical conception, but he does not concur if "historical conception" means simply scientific objectivity or neutrality and the claim — clearly impossible in concrete terms — to do without philosophy. "The determination of the essence is without doubt a purely historical task. But 'purely historical' means a whole conception of the world... The determination of the essence develops out of the method and spirit of empirical-inductive historiography, but it is a higher level task because it is situated at the point where empirical-inductive history becomes the philosophy of history".[20] Troeltsch thus accepts the primacy of the historical conception (in which Protestantism and the modern scientific orientation meet), in place of the Catholic primacy of revelation and the Church (which, according to Troeltsch, still dominates the thought of Loisy), but he develops it in a different way from Harnack. This is not only because, as a philosopher, he is more interested in clarifying the presuppositions of this historical method and in constructing a specific hermeneutical approach, but also because, by re-establishing links with philosophy, he is led to consider the speculative interpretations of Hegelianism of the figure of a human God, the coming of the Kingdom etc. as legitimate developments in the course of Protestant demythologisation: "So the idea of the human God could, for example, be identified as the essence, which initially appeared in a symbolic and visible form in the person of Jesus, which then developed,

---

[18] WH, pp. 395-96.
[19] WH, p. 397.
[20] WH, pp. 397-98.

in dogmatics and the philosophy of religion, as the doctrine of the Trinity and as Christology, though still enwrapped in a mythical form, and has finally been realised definitively in the modern theory of the unity of the divine spirit and the finite spirit and of its realisation in the development of spirit as such... Perhaps an analagous dialectical evolution could also be constructed for the idea of the Kingdom of God — from the eschatological preaching of Jesus, through the dogma of the Church and of the love of the human God, up to the modern concept of a kindgom of spirits united in God, or, up to a modern Christian-social ethic — if the biblical idea of the Kingdom of God be thought more fitting to express the essence than the Christology of the dogma of the primitive Church and of Paulinism".[21]

Troeltsch attaches an aristocratic connotation to the idea of a modern Christianity, in the sense of Protestantism: doubt and uncertainty, but also choice and responsibility, belong irreversibly to modern life, and we can consider the Catholic cult of authority as historically and psychologically inferior: "In it the original idea is brought down to the average level of the mass of men, to their mediocrity, and is contaminated with alien elements of ancient popular religion, of sacramental sacerdotal and sacrificial cult, of ancient mysticism and of an ever-present underlying popular superstition".[22] In fact, the historical or Protestant conception is inevitably subjective. If the determination of the essence aims not only at being *"an abstraction from phenomena"* but also *"a critique of phenomena"* (*"this critique consists not only in measuring what is not yet brought to fulfilment with the ideal acting within it, but also in discriminating between what conforms with the essence and what contrasts with it"*), then "in this way the part played by personal, incomprehensible considerations, which were already implicit in the idea of such a wide historical abstraction, increases even more". Here the relativistic considerations deriving from Dilthey that we found in *The Absoluteness of Christianity* reappear, and yet Troeltsch continues to express himself in the language of an idealistic philosophy of history ("the imperfection of the essence that is not yet fully clear about itself").[23]

In the work of Troeltsch, the converging towards a common determination of the essence, on the basis of rationally controllable means that are not constricted by any authority, is always sustained by a philosophical-theological vision that identifies the essence as origin and goal of the historical process. It is without doubt out of a need for truth, for

[21]   WH, pp. 402-403.
[22]   WH, p. 405.
[23]   WH, pp. 406-407.

scientific honesty, that he so often insists on the inevitable subjective conditioning of every inquiry and also that he appeals to history, a discipline with a complex methodological framework, with well-tried and rigorously controlled procedures, to find an antidote to that subjectivism. It seems to me that the same need leads him to consider as definitive the illuministic criticism of metaphysical or dogmatic constructions; this means that it is an existing situation, which we simply have to acknowledge, that determines the historical conception: "only the dissolution of every dogmatic constriction, resulting from a number of more general causes, first led us to concern ourselves with the determination of the essence. This attempts, in fact, to promote that interior unification and concord which is only possible once the authority of dogmas has been broken down".[24]

Thus Troeltsch saw truth above all in a scientific sense: for example, he wrote in *The Absoluteness of Christianity* that "in this book the question is one of truth, not of theology, and truth is taken to be accessible only on the basis of universally applicable scholarly methods".[25] In the essay we are examining he states that in the modern scientific study of history "there are thus sufficient guarantees that the opinion has coherent and uniform presuppositions and that the serious, conscientious intention to find truth that emerges for present time will also lead to uniform results".[26] But he also concerned himself with truth in an eschatological sense, the truth that awaits us in the future and which could differ to a greater or lesser degree from historical Christianity. Let us not forget that his conception of history assigns to Christianity the highest place, comparatively speaking, in the succession of divine revelations; but in all this there remains a degree of uncertainty, given the scarsity of our knowledge, and the definitive truth, the complete and absolute truth, could surpass even Christianity. "We are on the course and in the movement of life that leads to the Absolute when we dedicate ourselves to the living world of personalistic religion and perceive in Christianity its embodiment in our cultural context and our moment of history".[27] In this way, however, we could end up by constructing something as "essence" that has nothing to do with historical Christianity:

---

[24] WH, p. 438. Cf. "L'Aufklärung dans la théologie", *Recherches de Sciences religieuses* 72:3 (1984). The "subjectivity of the modern way of thinking" was the theme of Dilthey's that Troeltsch always kept in mind. Cf. W.Dilthey, *Gesammelte Schriften*, I (Leipzig und Berlin: Teubner 1923), p. 413.

[25] AC, p. 171. Cf. A. Loisy, *Autour d'un petit livre* (Paris: Picard, 1903) (abbreviation PL), p. 219: "Authentic truth has one interest only: truth itself".

[26] WH, p. 437.

[27] AC, pp.128-29. Cf. p. 116.

"We do not go recklessly in search of this risk, but the religious crisis of the present time drags us into the struggle... The men who concern themselves with these things are, despite any faults they may have, nevertheless men with a real thirst for truth, and the untenability of such a position would not long remain hidden from them".[28] Clearly here he is again alluding to scientific practice and to the honesty of the historian, but also to his looking forward to a definitive truth which could arrive in the future, but which today does not present itself separately from Christian forms of culture. "In this direction we can see the future that we are capable of foreseeing... At any rate, in this way we remain closely bound to the vital religious forces of our world and we abide by what the historical moment shows us to be the truth of Christianity. In the end, it is a question of truth and not Christianity, and it is certain that we have not yet reached the point where religious truth is to be found beyond the truth of Christianity".[29] But "religious truth", which is what is being spoken of here, is a philosophical truth: not truth that is "accessible only on the basis of universally applicable scholarly methods" but a universal essence of religion, which reveals itself progressively in the course of history.[30]

This brings us to our conclusion. Around what Harnack said Troeltsch constructed a complex and informed hermeneutic; it seeks the essence in the past (on the basis of the expectations of the present, and of the attempts to grasp a "religion of the future" through the processes of interiorisation and demythologisation that are already underway) and in the future (through a systematic questioning of the time of the origins). We must always bear in mind this reciprocal implication or circularity, which removes the

---

[28] WH, p. 439.

[29] WH, p. 446.

[30] See the radical criticisms of Gogarten in his essay *Historismus* of 1924: "It is by no means casual... that at the point in which Troeltsch says that without the thought of God there are no units of measure, he blandly adds: or something like it. This reveals with amazing clarity the purely idolatrous and visionary element of this (and not only this) philosophy of history" (cf. *Zwischen den Zeiten*, 1924, no. 8, pp. 7-25; republished in J. Moltmann [ed.], *Anfänge der dialektischen Theologie*, Part II [München: Chr. Kaiser Verlag, 1963, 1967]). What results from this equation between religious truth and philosophical truth is that the philosophy of religion is attributed with the role of founding knowledge; in concrete terms it acquires a threefold function: fundamental theology, theory of subjectivity, science of religion. Cf. G. Becker, "Die Funktion der Religionsphilosophie in Troeltschs Theorie des Christentums", in H. Renz, F.W. Graf (ed.), *Troeltsch-Studien. 3. Protestantismus und Neuzeit* (Gütersloh: Mohr, 1987) pp. 240-56.

past from historiographical objectivism and makes it a past *for us*, and removes the future from the tyranny of waiting or of human inventions and roots it in a past that is known. If Troeltsch criticised Harnack for having kept himself too close to primitive Christianity in the determination of the essence, it is perhaps not because he interpreted the problem in a fundamentally different way, but because he wanted to stress the hermeneutic circularity with a critical decisiveness grounded in the present and in the future. "We must therefore ask ourselves the following question: *what, in the period of the origins, contains that which is truly classic?...* What arose out of the proto-Christian missionary preaching, which is documented for eternity in the writings of the New Testament, was not pure Christianity, but Catholicism. It is undeniable that in those writings the conditions for the Catholic substitution of history with dogma are already implicit. The determination of the essence must therefore take second place to these writings and must reconstruct the historical preaching and the historical personality of Jesus on the basis of them. In fact, they alone constitute the truly decisive and essential element in the period of the origins". This, in the end, is simply what Harnack thought, but it needed to be made explicit that "the period of the origins must always be considered in the light of later development but this, in its turn, must always be considered on the basis of the period of the origins".[31]

What did Troeltsch think of Alfred Loisy? This question interests us because the essay we have examined is also, in part, about Loisy. First Troeltsch gives an accurate summary of Loisy's position, whereby he criticises Harnack for a determination of the essence centred on primitive Christianity and not on the whole development of the Christian Churches: "Harnack's conception is not the historical picture of the process, but just one stage, or rather, the radical formulation of individualistic Protestantism, which is detaching itself from the collectivity of the Church... The immutable essence of Christianity cannot be constructed in this way, but consists merely in the totality of the living Church and its actions".[32] Of course, here the Catholic and the Protestant conceptions are in contrast: it is probably true that, in order to avoid taking Catholicism as the natural outcome of primitive preaching, Harnack is forced to go back to a "Gospel of Jesus" which is difficult to separate from the interpretations of faith, and which, moreover, as a moral message, speaks directly to the individual without the necessary

---

[31]   WH, pp. 414, 423.
[32]   WH, pp. 389-90.

mediation of a community.[33] But Loisy's continuism is suspect on other accounts, because he interprets everything as necessary and, on the basis of a certain positivism or evolutionism, the essence loses the discriminating characteristic of a judgement on what exists. "Loisy's objection to Harnack may even be justified when he contests the actual conception of essence in Harnack or the unilateral abstraction of the essence from the preaching of Jesus... But it is unjustified when he wants to replace the concept of essence with that of Church. This reveals a residue of the anti-historical, Catholic-dogmatic mentality".[34] In Troeltsch's opinion, Loisy's theory of necessary evolution aims to justify Catholicism as the principal means of historical development (Protestantism appears only "in as much as its relative right to exist as criticism of the harm done by the late Medieval Church is recognised"[35]); it comes perhaps from an idealistic influence ("In this way Ehrhard, and even more clearly Loisy, constructed the connection, making reference to the hegelian interpretation of the development of Christianity put forward by Caird"[36]), and much more extensively and more certainly from a positivist influence. Troeltsch recalled the neo-kantian and diltheyan distinction between "sciences of nature" and "sciences of the spirit", between "explanation" and "comprehension", and he developed it into a dualist epistemology which, with reference to history, conceived of two kinds of knowledge: on the one hand, what could be called the naturalistic knowledge of the "explanation" (involving a concept of necessity "in a psychological-causal sense", whereby, with regard to "empirical-inductive" history, "the connection of an event with the forces inherent in it that precede it" is established"), and the spiritual or authentically historical knowledge of the "comprehension" (involving a concept of necessity "in an ethical-

---

[33] See WC, pp. 278-79. Cf. also the interesting essay by K. Neufeld, "L'ecclésiologie de Harnack", in J. Greisch, K. Neufeld, C. Théobald, *La crise contemporaine. Du modernisme à la crise des herméneutiques* (Paris: Beauchesne, 1973) pp. 87-133.
[34] WH, p. 398.
[35] WH, p. 404.
[36] *Ibid.* This was also the opinion, in France, of L. de Grandmaison; in his review of *The Gospel and the Church* (*Etudes*, January 20, 1903, pp. 145-74) he believed Loisy to have little connection with Newman, whom he mentioned explicitly, and to be closer to the Hegelism of Caird. In a note Loisy had mentioned two authors: Newman and Caird, but in fact he knew little about Caird (in the first edition of his book he thought he was Anglican, whereas he was Presbyterian); he had read an article about him given to him by Hügel. Cf. E. Poulat, *Histoire, dogme et critique dans la crise moderniste* (Tournai: Casterman, 1979) (abbreviation HDC), pp. 143-46, 376.

teleological sense", because here the subject, on the plane of possibilities, decides responsibly "what the consequence intimately demanded by an idea should be"). Troeltsch's view is that Loisy conceived of and applied only the first form of necessity and therefore his determination of the essence says only what happened and not what is right. "Precisely for this reason Loisy's considerations about the necessity of Catholicism are certainly interesting and in the main accurate from a historical-inductive point of view. But they have nothing to do with the essence. The determination of the essence requires not only the divining abstraction, but, in it and with it, also an ethically and personally grounded critique, which confronts the phenomena with the essence".[37]

---

[37]   WH, pp. 410-11.

IV

Loisy's Criticism of Harnack and Sabatier

Troeltsch certainly was right in pointing out the limits of Loisy's concept of historicism, in particular the unilateral adherence to an empirical-causal model of a naturalistic kind and the lack of thorough hermeneutic considerations regarding the ethical or existential basis of historical research. Loisy extended the historical and psychological reductionism typical of the Protestant tradition to such an extent that towards the end of his life he believed that the Resurrection was a creation of the collective faith of the early Christian communities and that faith itself (note the reference to Harnack) was nothing but an attempt to "disrupt the natural order, apparently mechanical and inevitable, of existence".[1] Thus there were indirect references to kantian tradition in Loisy, although he certainly had never personally known either Kant or Hegel.[2] Then, too, Loisy was bound to the historical method, namely, the system of modern sciences and the approach underlying them, and his judgements were the result of his adherence to this system not a reference to the Church, tradition or dogma. He believed that historical research was legitimate in its own right and, if in the writings in which he defended himself from his adversaries all he seemed to do was to distiguish historical truth from dogmatic truth, he was nonetheless convinced that a historical treatment of Christianity should be made to prevail over the old interpretation grounded in scholastic

---

[1]   Cf. A. Loisy, *La naissance du christianisme* (Paris: Nourry, 1933), pp. 120-23. Also see *The Gospel and the Church* (henceforth referred to as GC), English translation by Ch. Home (London: Isbister & Company Limited, 1903) p. 272: "The face of the world is twofold. Man is placed between nature, where all seems inevitable, and consciousness, where all appears free".

[2]   Cf. E. Poulat, CM, pp. 185-88.

metaphysics.[3] He therefore accepted the Protestant view whereby sacred history was not to be considered as distinct from secular history and that both should be subject to the same method of analysis. This emphasis on method points to the basic philosophic approach of a scholar who, like Harnack, wanted to be only an historian. Stirred to action by the consequences of this approach, the Catholic Church attacked it on intellectual grounds, countering with its traditional, scholastic and realist arguments. This clash had both negative and positive implications. The negative ones resulted from the attempt to impose a philosophy of the past on modern man — a philosophy that had no doubt been great but that had become alien to the interests and thought of the society of the time. Not to mention that this was attempted in a generally "anti-modern" climate with very serious political and ideological implications.[4] The positive ones were such in so far as they served as a reminder that a methodical prior selection of the aspects of reality can neither impede nor influence the mystery of being or the richness of its manifestations to humanity. Indeed, gnoseological realism also means that there is always a further step to be taken in our relations with the world (and ultimately with God), that it is impossible to exhaust the real by filtering it through the rules of knowledge.

This discussion was not and is not merely gnoseological. It entails profound moral and theological implications in its arguing for a scientific dominion over the world (where things exist to the extent that they are manifest and they must be manifest in the ways dictated by method) or for attention to the hidden aspects of reality. Loisy knew that in this respect

---

3   Cf. the letters to Blondel (February-March 1903) published by R. Marlé in *Au coeur de la crise moderniste. Le dossier inédit d'une controverse* (lettres de M. Blondel, H. Bremond, Fr. von Hügel, A. Loisy...) (Paris: Aubier-Montaigne, 1960) chapter III, pp. 70-113 (henceforth referred to as CCM).

4   Historicism, atheism and Germanism were seen as related but in a negative sense. In France a return to authentic French or Latin culture was invoked, as if this meant only Thomism (and monarchy in politics) and not the French Revolution and the Enlightenment. Or, perhaps it was believed that the Revolution and the Enlightenment had become part of the new methods of historical inquiry propounded by Protestantism and liberal culture, and that they could not or should not be introduced into France again. The two countries after all were in a state of constant hostility aggravated by recent wars. Loisy thus was considered a traitor by conservatives and nationalists. It is necessary however to distinguish doctrinal concerns (because as we shall see Loisy did not succeed in developing a historical method suited to the truth it was meant to serve) from traditionalist and anti-democratic concerns. His critics often failed to note this distinction.

science does not have the last word, but he did not re-establish the potential of metaphysics (as did many others of his generation who were sensitive to the debate briefly sketched here).[5] He relied instead on a form of mysticism for all that went beyond the plane of scientific objectivism (in this connection he seems to have been influenced by Lachelier's Kantianism) but this could still appear another way of stating that what is not an object of science is inconceivable and inexpressible — of stopping at an apparent dualism whose only aim was to make way for historical research.[6]

---

[5]   I am referring mainly to those who, in an anti-modernist sense, recover the relation with Greek culture and as a result certain beliefs that are taught by the Catholic Church to this day: for example, a metaphysical notion of being (in which the Aristotelian conception and the biblical conception would appear to coincide), gnoseological realism, and a purely rational demonstrability of the existence of God and the soul. A purely historical conception, however, eliminates all these points. Cf. G. Forni, "Tra modernismo e neotomismo: la 'filosofia cristiana' (1927-1933)", *Filosofia e teologia*, 1989, no. 2, pp. 387-410, and 1990, no. 1, pp. 175-97. With regard to these issues in Catholic philosophy, see: G. Saitta, *Le origini del neo-tomismo nel XIX secolo* (Bari: Laterza, 1912); G. Michelet, "La renaissance de la philosophie chrétienne", in *La vie catholique dans la France contemporaine* (Paris: Bloud et Gay, 1918) pp. 305-385; H. Duméry, "La philosophie catholique en France", in *L'activité philosophique contemporaine en France et aux Etats-Unis*, edited by M. Farber, vol. II (Paris: PUF, 1950); L. Foucher, *La philosophie catholique en France au XIX siècle avant la Renaissance thomiste et dans son rapport avec elle (1800-1880)* (Paris: Vrin, 1955).

[6]   Cf. E. Poulat, CM, pp. 188-204; also M. Vallois, *La formation de l'influence kantienne en France* (Paris, 1925; Genève: Slatkine Reprints, 1981), and P. Colin, "Le kantisme dans la crise moderniste", in *Le modernisme* (Paris: Beauchesne, 1980) pp. 9-81. Several critics have dwelt on the dualism in Loisy: Abbot Maignen in his articles in *La Verité française* (October 1903), and Abbot Gaudeau in the *Revue du clergé français* ("L'Eglise et l'Evangile", March 15, 1904, pp. 113-23; cf. E. Poulat, HDC, pp. 197-99, 231-33). Loisy argued that there is "a clear cut separation between theology and history... history sought facts, quantifiable and traceable data that could be rationally demonstrated; whereas theology was concerned with ineffable and supernatural truths having no direct connection with objective reality. Natural fact was the object of research, supernatural events the object of faith. The Christian as a believer could accept events undemonstrable by the scientist: he could believe what he risked denying, or ignoring, as an historian" (M. Guasco, "Teologia e storia della chiesa", in *Dizionario teologico interdisciplinare* [Casale Monferrato: Marietti, 1977] vol. I, p. 245). It is well-known that later, in opposition to this stand, Pope Pious X and the theologians of the time demanded not only that the supernatural should become an object of history, but also that the task of the Church historian should be to discover the presence of God or the signs of the supernatural event in history without rejecting the modern scientific method. This may certainly seem paradoxical unless it is taken as a request to

In the six articles Loisy wrote from 1898 to 1900 for the *Revue du clergé français* under the pen name Firmin, he opposed the individualism and the abstractness of the Protestant stance, in particular Harnack's (whose *Grundriss der Dogmengeschichte* had been translated into French by Fischbacher in 1893) and Sabatier's (who in 1897 had just published his *Outlines of a Philosophy of Religion*).[7] "Never has religion been conceived as a wholly personal matter of the individual, a mere psychological exercise in which each individual is both subject and judge. The direct and constant relationship established by religion between God and man has always been seen as implying at the same time an affective relationship between man and his fellow men. To say religion is to say the opposite of individualism. Religion in all its forms, even the imperfect ones, has always sought the union of man in God, not only the union of man and God... Therefore all that has gone under the name of religion throughout history has been, in one way or another, an institution".[8] The Protestants insisted on the ethical or interior character of religion and, hence, they inclined towards psychological reduction. Influenced by the Catholic conception of tradition and Church (as Troeltsch had rightly seen), Loisy highlights the social character and in this respect he seems to have been inspired also by positivist

---

rethink the historical method according to the needs of theology. With reference to the contemporary situation, Guasco wrote: "If the theologian cannot ask the historian to provide proof of the truth of an *event of faith* in that this evidence can only have a phenomenological basis, he can however ask him not to demonstrate the impossibility of the same event of faith using the tools at his disposal. It would be very improper to go from a statement like: 'it is not possible to demonstrate the historical value of certain narrations, the historical character of certain facts cannot be demonstrated, they cannot be called historical in the strict sense of the term' to the affirmative statement: 'these facts are outside the realm of experimental history, they are antihistorical'" (op. cit., pp. 256-57). This conclusion denotes an uncertain grasp on theory and the lack of in-depth analysis as it does not define the meaning of "fact" or "historical reality".

[7]   This does not mean that German or Protestant culture is seen in a negative light; quite the contrary, it was an important reference point for the French historian. Cf. PL, p. XVI: "What opened up before him was an immense field of study, the scope of which he could only guess from the education he had received; it was the work, incomplete yet impressive, accomplished by Protestant and rationalist exegesis...".

[8]   Cf. A. Firmin, "La théorie individualiste de la religion", *Revue du clergé français*, January 1, 1899, pp. 202-214.

or evolutionary tendencies.[9] The debate that ensued as to whether or not Loisy's thought could be reduced to Protestant positions centers on this problem. What they have in common is the primacy accorded to history and the tendency to demythologize, although anthropological reduction in Loisy is not of an individualistic kind but sociological and positivist, thereby approaching the positions of Catholicism.[10]

In opposition to Sabatier, Loisy then sets out to treat a fundamental hermeneutic theme for which Troeltsch too showed great interest: the difference between truth, which is always transcendent, and doctrine, historical and relative, which aims to express it. Of course, the Protestants also oppose ascribing a sacred character to doctrinal formulas, symbols and images. Rather, they think in terms of progress, of an evolution that will remove us from this sphere of the manifestation of the divine: moralization, interiorization. Loisy, by contrast, believes that this tendency transforms religion into philosophy and that in any case the human condition is such as to require that the acquisition of truth be mediated. "Our firmest ideas about religion are nothing more than metaphors and symbols, a sort of algebraic notation that represents inexpressible quantities". One cannot escape symbolic or metaphorical representation, and the attempt to do so leads to an even more dubious (philosophical) conceptual representation. "Although the idea of God could have humble origins, according to our way of thinking, this did not prevent religion from becoming great... The idol itself is the sign of divine presence. Whatever one does, there is no religion without images and symbols. The highest thought that man is able to have of God is still nothing more than an image, an idol in the primary sense, in which he seeks to situate the infinite". In this respect Sabatier sought to eschew historical and doctrinal

---

9   Loisy's relationship with the sociological school and with Durkheim has not to date been studied. What seems certain, however, is that Loisy's concept of the social character of religion differed from Durkheim's; as he states in these early articles, Loisy refused to incorporate religion into society. (cf. A. Firmin, "La definition de la religion", *Revue du clergé français*, April 1, 1899, pp. 193-209).
10 In this regard L. de Grandmaison wrote: "We would have a more accurate idea of the modernist spirit if we said that its supporters, dissatisfied with the traditional approach to dogmatic truth and struck by the incontestable disproof, provided by the whole of nineteenth century thought, of Protestant religious individualism, struggled to preserve the *psychology* and *sociology* of Catholicism at the expense of what we should not hesitate to call its *metaphysics*" (L. de Grandmaison, *Christus. Manuel d'histoire des religions* [Paris: Beauchesne, 1912] pp. 983-84; cit. by E. Poulat, HDC, p. 100).

mediation, but what he was proposing as the foundation of religion (the "sentiment of the divine") runs the risk of being totally arbitrary and of making a psychical state pass for "revelation".[11]

Like the Protestants, Loisy too acknowledged that religion evolved or progressed, after the pattern already noted in Troeltsch, from a multiplicity (from "the sheer chaos of bizarre, wavering, changing opinions of childish and gross superstitions") to higher forms characterized by unity, morality and so on. "One single, essential reform including a series of secondary reforms and advances made with great difficulty ends with an outcome as perfect as can possibly be achieved in the human condition: it begins with Moses, closes with Jesus and is perpetuated in the Church". Yet the sense of development cannot be that of a liberation from symbols or images because the divine as such is inaccessible, inexpressible, and the forms in which it manifests itself to man are ever-changing yet on the whole cannot be eliminated (in this respect one may speak of Loisy's "re-mythologization" in conformity with his mysticism and with the traditional claims of Catholicism). On the other hand Harnack and Sabatier cannot be endorsed when they postulate actual laws or phases which are necessary to historical development: "The supposed law of religious evolution has been up to now only a hypothesis or theory... It may offer advantages as to the classification of observed facts, but one must avoid taking it as a necessary rule or the infallible program of religious development since it is impossible to demonstrate its continual application throughout history".[12]

As Loisy states in the 1914 preface, *The Gospel and the Church* (1902) was intended as an anti-Protestant work, its critical emphasis on the so-called "essence of Christianity" of the liberal school, although it also broke with the official teaching of the Catholic Church, which it proposed to reform. It may be seen as bordering on pragmatism because in it the personal character of the divine was asserted with a view towards an educational and moral intent. At any rate, it supported an evolutionary philosophy in that it posited a spiritual development of humanity which the Church itself could promote through reform: "... it is up to the Church to decide whether it wants to or whether it can forget enough of its past and correct its excessive expectations to ensure its future by working efficaciously for the

---

[11]   Cf. A. Firmin, "L'idée de la révélation", *Revue du clergé français*, January 1, 1900, pp. 250-71; "La religion d'Israël", *Revue du clergé français*, October 15, 1900, pp.337-63.

[12]   Cf. A. Firmin, "La religion d'Israël", cit.

progress of humanity".[13]

Loisy does not wish to "refute" Harnack's work but simply "to determine its exact historical position"; he does not aim to demonstrate the "truthfulness" of the Gospel or of Catholic Christianity but simply "to analyze and define the bonds that unite the two in history".[14] Yet he immediately accuses Harnack of having imposed a theory on facts; to be a historian means "dealing with facts as they appear from evidence intelligently investigated, without introducing one's own conceptions into the texts explored, and (being) able to take account of the change that the ideas of past time inevitably undergo when adapted to modern thought".[15]

This marks the start of Loisy's effort to prove that his approach was "more historical" (more neutral and more impartial in the sense of a historiographical objectivism which Troeltsch rightly criticized) than his Protestant colleagues. In the process he encounters a series of difficulties and contradictions which appeared only at the beginning of the century but which some (like Troeltsch) were already better equipped to handle philosophically. Loisy distinguished between the task of the theologian and that of the historian, and so he argued, as we have seen, that while the historian must consider the past as past, the theologian has the right to actualize, to translate the original mythical element. Instead it is through having conceived a historical theology that the Protestants achieved their results: actualization does not contradict the historicity of the object but becomes in fact a consitutive element of it. Loisy, at least at first, was far from dealing with these hermeneutical problems of circularity (also because these problems would have inevitably required a more radical theoretical independence on his part) and in the system of double-column bookkeeping[16] he saw, as an historian, that the Protestants' calculations did not tally because their actualizations were too radical and untenable. In short, Loisy accused them of seeing everything in the light of the present and of the ideas of the present: since these ideas are, as Sabatier had observed,

---

[13]   Cf. *L'Evangile et l'Eglise* (Paris: Nourry, 1929[5]; designated EE) pp. 2-6. This is the definitive version published in 1902-03 (the chapter, "Evangelical sources", was added in the 1903 edition), with a new preface dated 1914 preceding the introduction (this preface is not in the English edition - designated GC-published in 1903).

[14]   EE, p. VII; GC, pp. 2-3.

[15]   EE, p. XI; GC, p. 5.

[16]   The expression is used by Abbot Maignen (articles in *La Vérité française*, October, 1903), cf. E. Poulat, HDC, p. 197.

science and morals, Christianity would have to become moralized and interiorized so as to clear the way for science's claims upon the world. In other words, he clearly perceived the neo-kantian division between faith and science in liberal thinking and perhaps also a hint of philosophical post-Christianity (which indeed there was) because what interested him instead was the reconstitution of the past as such and the whole evolutionary span that reaches us through the Catholic Church. "At bottom, Sabatier and Harnack have wished to reconcile Christian faith with the claims of science and of the scientific spirit of our time. The claims must indeed have become great, or be believed to be great, for the faith has become very small and modest... Religion is thus reconciled with science, because it no longer encounters it. This trust in the goodness of God either exists in a man or it does not; but it seems impossible for a sentiment to contradict any conclusion of biblical or philosophical criticism".[17] Yes, but this methodical separation is in fact what institutes, from the outset of the modern age, the field of science as a universal causal link free of faith and miracles and completely subject to its own laws; it is on history as science, as a part of science, that the Protestants relied and so Loisy's criticisms suggest — though they do not realize — the construction of a different kind of historicity.

What then did Loisy believe was the "essence of Christianity"? Not what appears as essential today, or what it appeared to be after the Reformation, but what every age has considered it to be: "If any common features have been preserved or developed in the Church from its origin till today, these features constitute the essence of Christianity. At least, the historian can take account of no others; he has no right to apply to Christianity a method that he could not apply to any other religion whatsoever".[18] Considering the essence in this way removes from it the critical or discriminant meaning regarding what exists, which Troeltsch on the other hand points out as being typical of the Protestant standpoint; continuity and constancy prevail. And this is what appears as the essence to the true historian who does not superimpose a theory on data. But the true historian is, in Loisy's view, free from faith and so he treats the so-called events of salvation according to whether or not they can be confirmed empirically. A philosophical basis is also retained, which in this case is an evolutionary vision of history. Loisy's continuistic approach therefore links Christianity to Judaism again ("It is, therefore, in the highest degree arbitrary to decide that Christianity in its essence must be all that the Gospel has not

---

[17]   EE, p. XII; GC, p. 6.
[18]   EE, p. XV; GC, p. 9.

borrowed of Judaism, as if all that the Gospel has retained of the Jewish tradition must be necessarily of secondary value") and also shows the weaknesses in Harnack's approach, which have already been pointed out: "Whatever we think, theologically, of tradition, whether we trust it or regard it with suspicion, we know Christ only by the tradition, across the tradition, and in the tradition of the primitive Christians. This is as much as to say that Christ is inseparable from His work, and that the attempt to define the essence of Christianity according to the pure Gospel of Jesus, apart from tradition, cannot succeed, for the mere idea of the Gospel without tradition is in flagrant contadiction with the facts submitted to criticism".[19]

It should be noted that, although Loisy reassesses tradition, unlike the Protestants he does not explain the relation between history and tradition. To use his own words, if we do not "trust" tradition, namely, the Church, it is impossible to recover an image of Christ; for it is thus that we have life, movement and development, and not a static essence.[20] How then could history as science oppose the tradition of the Church? How could there be a historical truth and a dogmatic truth? These oppositions, however, lose their impact in Loisy because history takes in all the phases or aspects of Christian evolution, and tradition is cognizant of the relativity of the formulas and of the transcendence of truth, setting aside the intellectualistic or fixed approach.[21] To define this character of reality, Loisy refers to the essence as to a living organism which, though growing and developing according to a plan, does not change its own principle. On the contrary, this principle is realized more fully in history. "Why not find the essence of Christianity in the fullness and totality of its life, which shows movement and variety just because it is life, but inasmuch as it is life

---

[19]   EE, pp. XVII-XXI; GC, p. 13.

[20]   "Harnack seems also to fear that his essence of Christianity might be spoiled if he introduced into it any idea of life, of movement and development" (EE, p. XXIII; GC, p. 14).

[21]   In the Catholic Church at the time it was feared that the pragmatic and vitalist tendencies widepread in European culture would cause theology to view doctrinal or dogmatic issues as irrelevant; this was a decisive aspect in the struggle against modernism and in the restoration of Thomism. In effect the historical significance of these tendencies is not univocal: within the framework of theology and religious philosophy they oppose intellectualism, abstraction and the separation between science and life of the traditional conceptions. However the conditions in modern industrial societies are such that the aspect of "movement", of religious activism may be accentuated without attaching sufficient importance to the problem of truth. Cf. A. Leclère, *Pragmatisme, modernisme, protestantisme* (Paris: Bloud, 1909).

proceeding from an obviously powerful principle, has grown in accordance with a law which affirms at every step the initial force that may be called its physical essence revealed in all its manifestations? Why should the essence of a tree be held to be but a particle of the seed from which it has sprung, and why should it not be recognized as truly and fully in the complete tree as in the germ?".[22] The image of the seed and the plant serves the purpose of refuting Harnack's purported "primitivism", his close link to the initial phase of Christianity (in the sense of a "return to the origins" proper to Protestant tradition: objectively speaking, however, Harnack's true position is a difficult and controversial one, as we have seen in the comparison with Troeltsch). Moreover, it serves to define the question of essence (which for Loisy is recognizable in the plant, in an already formed being) and to present the first outlines of the philosophy of history. "The particular and varied forms of the development, in so far as they are varied, are not of the essence of Christianity, but they follow one another, as it were, in a framework whose general proportions, though not absolutely constant, never cease to be balanced, so that if the figure change, its type does not vary, nor the law that governs its evolution".[23]

Loisy considered Protestant intellectual development essentially as a process which reduced the divine to the psychological or the philosophical. In this respect, he defended religion from neo-kantian interiorization, although as we have mentioned he inclined towards another form of reductionism, i.e. sociological Catholicism. "It might be said that the God of Harnack, driven from the domain of nature, driven also from history, in so far as history is made of facts and play of thoughts, has taken refuge on the heights of human conscience, and is now only to be seen by those who have keen perception... Can the conscience keep for long a God that science ignores, and will science respect forever a God that it does not know? Can God be goodness if He is not first life and truth?".[24] With these fundamental propositions Loisy probably posed more questions than he could answer and opened the door to issues that had apparently been given short shrift in his philosophical stance. The split between science and faith at the basis of modern scientific enquiry that Loisy himself endorsed appeared as typically Protestant to him and essentially oriented towards atheism; a God who is goodness or mercy, an ethical God in the harnackian sense, points in the same direction because, lacking an ontological

---

[22]   EE, p. XXVI; GC, p. 16.
[23]   EE, p. XXVIII; GC, p. 18.
[24]   EE, pp. XXXII-XXXIII; GC, p. 21.

foundation ("being and truth"), it is understood as a value or ideal, thus as an aspect of human consciousness. He accused Harnack of having driven God from history in that history is seen as "facts and play of thoughts". But was this not Loisy's position as well?

First of all, according to Loisy, we cannot deal with the fundamental documents of Christianity only from a textual or literary point of view; they cannot be severed from the tradition (society and institutions) of which they are an expression. This would perhaps result in considering abstractly the individual freely interpreting the text, and the text before him. Critical analysis must at any rate be conducted and in detail through the study of the religious movements within which those texts were shaped; in this respect the school of Tübingen was right.[25] The Gospels are therefore the partial expression of primitive Christianity, following the evolution of Christianity precisely because they are a product and testimony of Christianity.[26] Of course, this way of reasoning is turned mainly against Harnack, in particular against his distinction between the Gospel of Jesus and the Gospel about Jesus and against the possibility of tracing, on a historical and critical basis, an essence of Christianity untouched by ecclesiastical or institutional developments, an essence which could even become judge and regulator of all historical development. We have already found statements to this effect,[27] although even in Loisy's work we find a distinction like the one in Harnack expressed in terms of a relation between history and theology: there is progress in the Christological assertions in the Gospels that Loisy does not see as progress towards truth, or at least historical truth, but moves increasingly from this initial and relatively scant factual reality towards exaggeration or idealization. "Thus, little by little, there is formed in the atmosphere of faith, beyond what can be called the historical reality of the Gospel, beyond even its idealization to suit the Messiah, the dogma which aims at determining its providential meaning, its universal scope, its transcendent efficacy"[28]. Of course, the "Gospel about Jesus" does not carry the same weight for Loisy as it does for Harnack, because the former is far from regarding it as a deviation from the essence (because of his evolutionary, continuistic approach). Once we adopt the historical method as the only one, however, the development of Christological conceptions can be recorded as such, as a history of ideas or

---

25   EE, pp. 5-6; GC, p. 27.
26   EE, p. 15; GC, p. 35.
27   EE, p. XXI; GC, pp. 13-14.
28   EE, p. 26; GC, p. 46.

beliefs whose truth value is irrelevant to the historian: the Christ in history and the Christ of faith again tend to separate. "The subject of this faith is at no stage of its development presented to the historian as an actual reality. Criticism has not to decide if Jesus is or is not the Word Incarnate, if He existed before His terrestrial manifestation... Considered as belief, this idea is addressed to faith, that is to say, to the man judging with all his soul the worth of the religious doctrine presented to him. The historian as such need not constitute himself either apologist or adversary. He knows it simply as a conception...".[29]

In the second chapter Loisy deals with eschatology. His treatment of the subject naturally reflects the theoretical choices which have been pointed out, especially his refuting Harnack's attempt to demythologize the conception of the Kingdom seen as an interior, moral event detaching Christian hope from the Judaic doctrine of the Revelation. According to Loisy, the coming of the Kingdom may be the true essence of the Gospel,[30] whereas Harnack considers this aspect to be superficial and bound up with tradition and sees the true and new meaning of the Gospel (the kernel as opposed to the husk) in the faith in a merciful God the Father.[31] "The historian must resist the temptation to modernize the conception of the Kingdom";[32] Harnack, by contrast, actualizes and internalizes it, as it were, turning it into a reality or an ethical discovery disrupting the continuity between the Old Testament and the New. A pastoral and apologetic actualization is possible and perhaps necessary but this task, proper to the theologian, must not concern the historian, who instead must search for the original sense.[33] This difference appears to be more marked in eschatology because from an historical point of view the end of the world was felt as imminent, and so primitive Christianity expresses singular disdain of social organization, ethics and politics. However, in subsequent theological thought, conditioned by a certain disappointmnt of expectation, all these elements were to become determinant or rearranged differently.

Despite such profound transformations, however, the unity and the continuity of Christianity are ensured by tradition and the Church. Loisy accepts the relativity or mutability of historical events, beliefs and institutions because in his thought the conception of coherent development

---

[29] EE, pp. 30-31; GC, pp. 50-51. Cf. EE, pp. VI-VII, 105, 115-16.

[30] EE, p.39; GC, p. 59.

[31] EE, pp. 43-44; GC, p. 63.

[32] EE, p. 54; GC, p. 73.

[33] EE, pp. 26, 30-32; GC, pp. 46, 50-52.

provides a unifying effect on this dispersion, just as the idea of an essence of religion and the correlative idea of a constant anthropological structure did in Harnack. Sustained by a general evolutionary vision, Loisy can readily acknowledge relativity and hold his approach to be more strictly historical than Harnack's, which is dominated by radical actualizations and theoretical decisions. According to Loisy, it does not seem "that the Gospel is only addressed 'to the inner soul of man that is always the same'. The Gospel of Jesus is addressed to the whole man, to snatch him from the conditions normal to his present life".[34] The Gospel itself has always been intertwined with cultures and with different civilizations, and so it is senseless to conceive this relation only in terms of an opposition, or to think of a progress that would end up removing religion from history, which amounts to saying from the corporeity and humanity of the religious experience. "How far apart are the truth of history and the theory proposed with such ardour and conviction!". Loisy could still rail against Harnack,[35] trying to present himself as more of an historian than the great German scholar and so, in accordance with the ideals of his age, more truthful and credible.

The search for the past as past, which is the task of the historian, must first of all separate the figure of Christ from Harnack's firm actualizations. "It is not without some appearance of reason that the idea that Jesus regarded himself as the Messiah has been contested. Side by side with the confused idea, frequently held both now and formerly, of the Kingdom of Heaven, there could only be a conception equally vague of the Messiah; and just as the way out of the contradiction involved in the idea of the Kingdom seemed to lie in the denial of all that was least satisfying to the modern intelligence, namely, its eschatological character, so to escape from the difficulties presented by the conception of the Messiah, it has been thought well to suppress it, or at least subordinate it entirely to the conception formed of the Son of God".[36] Hence we may speak of Loisy's re-mythologization, which appears as authentically historical, as opposed to the philosophical subjectivism of the Protestant tradition: "It is his own religion, not that of the Gospel, which Harnack expounds and defends, when he announces that 'God and the soul, the soul and its God are the whole contents of the Gospel': the historical Gospel has none of this mystic and individualistic character... The historian sees no reason for this violent

---

[34]   EE, p. 64; GC, p. 82.
[35]   EE, p. 66; GC, p. 83.
[36]   EE, pp. 81-82; GC, pp. 98-99.

interpretation".[37] The reason that Loisy does not see, however, is clear enough: he feels bound to early Christianity through the tradition of the Church despite the fact that this Christianity had become largely extraneous and incomprehensible because written in mythological terms. The Protestants who want to go back directly to the origins are more keenly aware of the cultural distance and try to overcome it by establishing the essence, by separating the absolute from the relative, which strikes Loisy as a pointless philosophical distinction. "But who then has distinguished in the conception of the Kingdom the idea of an inner Kingdom which is to have an absolute value, and the idea of a Kingdom that is to come whose value is to be held only relative? Who has found in the filial consciousness of Christ an element of universal scope, namely, the knowledge of God the Father, and a Jewish element of which the sole advantage was to define Jesus in history, namely, the idea of the Messiah?... He who wishes to decide historically the thoughts of the Saviour has not first to discover what can suit the mind of man today, or what can be held to be unchanged".[38] It is not a question of separating the absolute and the relative, but of ackowledging the fundamental paradox, namely, that "the entire Gospel is bound up with a conception of the world and of history that is no longer ours; but it is the whole Gospel and not only its imagined essence, which is not 'inseparably' bound" which has been handed down to us through the mediation of the Church.[39]

As we have seen, Loisy defended a certain notion of symbol (against the Protestants who appeared to him as moving towards a philosophical dissolution of Christianity) as the necessary expression of religious faith. Humanity has aspirations which tend to the infinite but can only fulfil them in a finite form. Moreover, this form cannot be conceptual but only imaginative and symbolic, otherwise it would lose its effectiveness. We must not, therefore, reject the Jewish element, as if it were an avoidable limitation, because it belongs to the dimension of the Incarnation, of the communicative expression of an otherwise fleeting and inaccessible truth. If Jesus really was a man, He had to belong to a certain population, to speak from within a certain civilization. But this aspect, already noted by Harnack, takes on a positive sense here because Judaism (the idea of the Kingdom or that of the Messiah) is the human body of an eternal spirit; instead of being an obstacle, it is the only means that truth has chosen to be

---

[37]   EE, p. 92; GC, p. 109.
[38]   EE, pp. 93-94; GC, pp. 110-111.
[39]   Cf. EE, pp. 97-99; GC, p. 114.

communicated to humanity of all times. Otherwise, if this body were lost, we would also lose the spirit and truth; the Gospel as a metaphysical possibility, as an invisible essence, is not something that can be comprehended or experienced by humanity.[40]

Through this conception of the symbolic Loisy believed he had done justice to the reality of Christianity and to the claims of historical science by restoring the evolutionary stratification of various cultures. It is in fact probably an error, typical of modern apologetics, to want to see the expressions of primitive faith as proof of the fundamental events of salvation. The assertions of the primitive Christians are not meant to be the empirical evidence of a historical fact, but the communicative incarnation, the *symbol* of the religious faith which gives shape and interior efficacy to the truth. For example, in the case of the "message of Easter" (the announcement of the empty tomb and of the apparitions of Christ) and of the "faith of Easter" (in the Resurrection), we cannot say that the content or the object of faith is a "fact" in the sense of historical science, nor that evidence of this fact can be found in the message. The disappearance of a body can be explained in many ways (and all of them are more acceptable to the historian than the one provided by Christians), and the same can be said about the appearances: "Christ risen from the dead does not belong to the order of the present life, which is that of sensible experience, and consequently the resurrection is not a fact that can have been directly and formally established".[41]

Besides this superimposition of a pseudo-scientific mentality and regardless of its outcome, however, we can reconsider the faith-message relation not as a particularization of the fact-proof relation, but as a hermeneutic, symbolic relation in which the message is the expression or the incarnation of faith. "The faith of the apostles is not the message (of Easter); it comes direct from the ever-living Christ, and hails Him as such. Compared with this faith, the imaginative representation or theoretical conception of the resurrection, the character of the appearances, are secondary matters. However, the faith is not independent of the message". The last statement returns to the anti-Protestant debate in that the faith in the ever-living Christ cannot be separated from the expressive form it has

---

[40]   Cf. EE, pp. 103-104; GC, p. 121.

[41]   EE, pp. 115-116; GC, p. 131. Loisy still uses expressions which are paradoxical and untenable from a scientific point of view, such as "supernatural reality" and "supernatural fact" and then declares that these realities are not completely subject to empirical or experimental proof (EE, p. 117; GC, p. 131).

assumed in humanity: "Harnack desires to keep the essence and not the form, the faith without its proof, which he judges obsolete. Perhaps he is mistaken in taking for a mere proof that which in the apostolic writings is above all an expression of faith... It is a mistake to oppose the faith, as an absolute thing, to the message and call the message relative: the faith has lived, and still lives, in the message, which is even its reality, in so far as it is an attempt to communicate the faith".[42]

The Church is a living body which has had to develop certain organs, change its overall equilibrium in order to save itself and the truth with which it had been entrusted: "Such, as a matter of fact is the law of all development, and the natural growth of living things knows similar experiences... The Church can fairly say that, in order to be at all times what Jesus desired the society of His friends to be, it had to become what it has become: for it has become what it had to be to save the Gospel by saving itself".[43] Loisy returns to the difference between primitive and historical Christianity as indicated by Harnack[44] to highlight neither corruption nor decadence of some kind but the necessary transformation leading to an original stratum, that of the expectation of the Kingdom, felt as imminent, to subsequent strata of organization, dogma and hierarchy: "Jesus foretold the Kingdom, and it was the Church that came". Nor, we are constantly reminded at every turn or with every particular, institutional or doctrinal aspect, could it have been otherwise; it could not have been any other way: "... all progress proceeds from what preceded it", according to a "de facto need that is coupled to logical needs", something which seems irreconcilable with Loisy's stand in his first articles in regard to the philosophy of history.[45]

What seems immediately clear, and it cannot be gainsaid, is that doctrinal formulas lack the certainty, the absoluteness and the perpetuity of the truth which is manifested in them; formulas are culturally or historically conditioned. However this problem cannot be treated in the terms we have already seen as the relation between fact and proof, event and testimony, faith and message. Or, at least, it is problematic to think of it in this way, given that we know absolutely nothing about fact or faith as such (apart from a communicative incarnation). In other words, we cannot

---

[42] Cf. EE, pp. 117-19; GC, pp. 134-35.
[43] EE, p. 136; GC, p. 150.
[44] "The society imagined by Christ, says Harnack, was something invisible and heavenly, because it concerned the inner life of man. Evangelical Christianity was as a soul without a body" (EE, p. 126; GC, p. 141).
[45] Cf. EE, pp. 152-53; GC pp. 164-65.

judge the truthfulness of a formula by measuring it with the very "thing" it is meant to express; rather it is to be measured inevitably against other formulas. This, according to Loisy, is the human condition — being always and anyhow in mediation, in a language determined case by case.[46] Yet a posteriori elucidation of the content of faith is not an essentially scientific procedure which the individual historian applies to documents, or better, to their historical stratification, as the Protestants erroneously maintain; they fail to see the collective dimension and therefore the practical and vital dimension of interpretation. "Is the Gospel of Jesus in principle individualist or collectivist? The question which seemed of prime importance to past centuries, namely, if the object of faith is to be determined by Scripture alone or by tradition with Scripture, retires into the background".[47]

Language, history and society in the production of doctrine and dogma: yes, but what remains of the absolute, the true, the authentic? In the maze of interpretations what is still there to tell us that God has entered into a relationship with man, and that He is still there? Nothing, apparently, and it remains to be seen whether such a radical statement of the human element of the formulas necessarily concerns only the historian (who is methodically free of faith and treats Christianity like any other religion) or also the theologian. Loisy, however, seems to be more interested in the aspects of dogmatic evolution than in the permanence of the truth expressed through them: truth is somehow presupposed, but in so far as it is inconceivable and inexpressible, it escapes the field of inquiry. "The conceptions that the Church presents as revealed dogmas are not truths fallen from heaven, and preserved by religious tradition in the precise form in which they first appeared. The historian sees in them the interpretation of religious facts, acquired by a laborious effort of theological thought. Though the dogmas may be divine in origin and substance, they are human in structure and composition".[48]

There are also different attempts to reconcile the absolute and the relative in dogmatic formulas. First of all the very notion of evolution and development, which has received such scant attention in the Catholic Church, should be developed more thoroughly. If a dogmatic definition were to be reached in this connection, it should insist on the "law of progress" that has governed the history of Christianity from the very outset. We could

---

[46] "Even the teaching and the appearance of Jesus have had perforce to be interpreted; the whole question is to know if the commentary is homogeneous with the text or heterogeneous" (EE, p. 170; GC, p. 181).

[47] EE, pp. 198-99; GC, p.209.

[48] EE, pp. 200-201; GC, pp. 210-211.

thus find a way out of the traditional situation in which the theologian alone is entrusted with defending the absolute character of dogma (leaving the non-believer to concern himself with the historical-evolutionary aspects) and to see how the opposition between the absolute and the relative can be resolved in theology.[49]

Another possible procedure has to do with the demythologization of the formulas, given that symbols and dogmatic definitions are relative to a certain state of knowledge or to visions of the world which then change and require (so that the formulas can continue to express completely and clearly what they mean and so preserve within them an element of identity) new interpretations of the doctrine that has been handed down. "In such a case, a distinction must be drawn between the material sense of the formula, the external image it presents, related to ideas received from antiquity, and its proper religious and Christian significance, its fundamental idea, which can be reconciled with new views of the constitution of the world and the nature of things in general". Christ's descent into hell and His ascent into heaven cannot be taken as a journey either underground or through the upper atmosphere, although this was literally believed for many centuries. On the other hand, the dogmatic sense remains the same, "because by them is always taught a transitory relation of the soul of Christ with the just under the ancient law, and the glorification of His risen humanity". According to Loisy, there is thus an "apparent sense" of the formulas, which changes continuously, and a "more spiritual idea" of their content: and so we are closer to Harnack's position than seemed possible at first since the demythologizing process separates the "husk", the changing, historical exterior, from the "kernel", the theological meaning or the fundamental idea. Is it not also said that in the conflict between the various visions of the world, the *spiritual* character of Christian truth emerges ever more clearly for it allows us still to believe the eschatological declarations of Jesus concerning an imminent end? One could, of course, point to the basic failure of Loisy's re-mythologization, since the multiplicity of the symbolic and the entire ancient vision of the world (see the discussion regarding the connection between Judaism and Christianity) are not the only and definitive expressions of truth. Could we think then, contrary to what was previously stated, that the faith-message relation has more than one dimension, or that the truth — per se interior and spiritual — is capable of various historical incarnations? What remains divergent is that for Loisy not even the conceptual element expresses the identity of Christianity; there

---

[49] EE, pp. 203-205; GC, pp. 215-17.

is no "essence", therefore our faith turns to something inexpressible through the relativity of myths and symbols, of meanings and of *ideas*. "It is not with the elements of human thought that an everlasting edifice can be built. Truth alone is unchangeable, but not its image in our minds. Faith addresses itself to the unchangeable truth, through a formula, necessarily inadequate, capable of improvement, consequently, of change".[50]

Faith-message, spirit-body, supranature-nature: these are different ways of saying that reality has two sides, two dimensions, although one always manifests itself to us (that of the message, the corporeity of the sign or symbol, which in this text appear as equivalent terms), and so we are forced, through the only one at our disposal, to reach the other, of which we can say nothing. This is how Loisy grasped the hermeneutic value of the concept of incarnation: by positing this parallelism and at the same time by denying that the spirit can be grasped outside the body, the supranature outside nature. Science, and historical science in particular, is the science never of divine but of human matters through which the divine is manifested. "If all movement whose sequence can be perceived is to be called natural, and if the nature of God's action in the soul, and the confident impulse of the soul towards God, are to be classed as outside nature, then Christian worship is natural in its external characteristics and coordinated to a supernatural effect, in so far as it acts on the soul by a sensible means to aid in producing that which is properly supernatural in man, namely, life in God". Of course what is being said here about worship also applies to the evangelical message: "The evangelical word, the indispensable means of faith, is just as natural as a text, as the sacraments are as a sign, but it is nonetheless the vehicle of a supernatural good".[51] Loisy is constantly driven to speak about what, according to his own principles, was beyond the field of observation. He did not realize, for example, that an investigation into the "confident impulse of the soul" could be entrusted to psychology and so be placed within the world of "nature", while what he meant to indicate with the expression, the relationship between man and God, escapes definition. He further altered the sense of his discourse by more broadly referring the dialectic of the sensible and of the spiritual, a dialectic rooted in religion, to linguistic communication as such, where it is instead evident that the physical incarnation through which meaning is manifest is not at all the visible side of the unseen world. Loisy however was primarily concerned with opposing the purely interior or spiritual worship

---

50   Cf. EE, pp. 206-209; GC, pp. 216-17.
51   EE, pp. 254-55; GC, pp. 258-59.

propounded by the Protestants by forcefully asserting the necessary corporeal mediation that must embody all truth for the human condition. "The same evangelist who gives the formula of worship in spirit, gives also the formula of the Incarnation; the two correspond to one another; God is a spirit, as is also His word; the true worship is spiritual, since it is founded on the communication of the Divine Spirit. But just as God the Spirit is made manifest in the Incarnate Word, so the life of the Spirit is communicated and maintained by spiritual sacraments".[52] But, precisely by embracing the Johannic conception of the Incarnation (divine-human, spiritual-sensible, heaven-earth), Loisy extends it analogically to the understanding of linguistic communication and sacramental action, in which instead the inaccessible sphere of the divine and the eternal is replaced by the more modest and, above all, more accessible sphere of meaning. "It is with the sacraments as with ordinary language, the virtue of ideas passes into the words, acts through the words, is communicated really, physically, by the words, and only produces its effect on the mind by the aid of the words. Therefore it is fair to speak of the virtue of words, for they contribute to the existence and fortune of ideas...".[53]

If Loisy insisted so much on the incarnate, historical and social dimension of religion, to what extent had Christianity become for him a religion of humanity, or of the future and progress?[54] It is evident first of all that the elevation of the human, effected by the descent of the divine into humanity, places the latter in a particular and unique position in Christianity: "Christianity is a religion, and a universal one, because it incarnates the sole God in the Son of man, and adores in God Man the God of all humanity".[55] But while the pagans ran the risk of confusing the worship of God and the worship of man, Christianity avoided that confusion while satisfying, through the worship of Christ, the need for deification, which

---

[52] EE, p. 256; GC, p. 260.

[53] EE, p. 257; GC, p. 261.

[54] I am referring of course to the text in question and to the beginning of this century and not to the later developments that this theme underwent in Loisy's work (an example may be found in the 1914 preface where Christianity and the Church seem subordinated to and, in a way, oriented toward the progress of humanity, cf. EE, pp. 5-6). His fundamental ideas however are already present in *L'Evangile et l'Eglise* and in *Autour d'un petit livre* (in particular as regards progress, science and the meaning of modernity, cf. PL, pp. XX-XXV, XXXIV-XXXV, 20, 48, 128-29, 150-54). See E. Poulat, CM chapter VII, and appendix of this book.

[55] EE, p. 251; GC, p. 255.

seems to be innate in humanity. Christ remains God and humanity is raised in Him to divinity. We might say that humanity adores itself in Jesus, although it is clear that it does not forget its own condition or God's.[56] Christianity is the result of a deep-rooted need, or rather, the need for a form of worship which deified humanity. Indeed, we see how the worship of a being, both human and divine, developed out of a rigorous monotheism, whose formula has never been abandoned. This tendency did not arise with Christ, it belongs instead to what may be called "primitive revelation", which has never been explicitly specified and which mankind has always borne in the depths of its religious consciousness: "The sole article that constitutes this unexplained revelation, that Jesus manifested in Himself and in His life as much as in His teaching, and was the first to show in a clear and intelligible manner because He realized it in Himself, is that God reveals Himself to man in man, and that humanity enters with God into a Divine association".[57]

The novelty of Christianity therefore is only relative. Christ revealed the eternal anthropological principle of religion which man had always believed but only vaguely understood. With Christ instead the mists of old mythologies are dissipated and the beauty and centrality of interior reality appears: "It is certain that the eternal principle of the passage of the Divine through the human then received a new application, very clear and very fruitful, that this application was the Christian religion and the worship of Jesus, and that it could be nothing else".[58]

---

[56] EE, p. 263; GC, p. 266.
[57] EE, pp. 264-65; GC, p. 268.
[58] EE, pp. 265-66; GC, p. 269.

V

Loisy's Second "Petit Livre"

The Gospel and the Church was a confutation of Harnack, although Harnack influenced Loisy much more than would appear from a cursory reading. Loisy drew a distinction between a substantive kernel of Christianity, which is what appears to history or to modern science, and a historically unreliable husk, which is the product of metaphysical or theological speculation. In short, a Christ of history and a Christ of faith: the former was accorded a certain amount of attention owing to the necessity of placing biblical revelation in the sphere of the real and the latter was relegated to the margins with a resulting decline in the interest in the Resurrection and the divinity.[1]

Although all Loisy wanted was to be considered an historian, he had fairly fixed views of science, progress and freedom.[2] He shared "... the aspirations of an age that moves forward leaving the Church far behind",

---

[1] If errors may be detected in his position, Loisy argues, it is because "what was a modest historical essay" was mistaken for "a system of theological doctrine". *The Gospel and the Church* was intended as a defense of all the traditional beliefs, but "in the light of history": "He employed the Gospels as historical documents... He observed that the Resurrection of Christ is not, strictly speaking, a historical fact and, in this respect, it cannot be demonstrated historically: he did not deny that Christ had risen... He limited himself to expounding the circumstances and the significance of the testimonies from an historical viewpoint, not touching upon what are matters of faith" (PL, pp. VII-VIII. All quotations from *Autour d'un petit livre* are translated by the translator). In this regard the correspondence between Loisy and Blondel from February to March 1903 is very important (*Autour d'un petit livre* was published at the beginning of October), CCM, pp. 0-113.

[2] "Ideas cannot be beaten to death with a stick" was his reaction to ecclesiastical censorship (PL, p. XXI).

although as a Christian he was keenly aware of the uneasiness of a Catholic culture that had not yet taken into account the sciences and the languages of modernity.[3] The Church and Christianity cannot be cut off from a modern world "... that seeks to live, to learn and to progress in every respect,"[4] even though this involved a difficult and complex transformation as, for instance, a renewal in theological studies against Scholasticism: "... today the world is asking us to explain God and Christ because our definitions are expressed in a language that in part differs from common usage".[5]

On the other hand (and this is a point on which Loisy and Harnack agree), the Scriptures remain sacred and inviolable even after being submitted to a critical scrutiny that elucidates their origin and composition. Indeed this scrutiny, which is demanded by "the general culture of our time", provides new tools and possibilities for biblical criticism. "Faith does not have a permanent abode on earth... Any attempt to confine it within what once was an edifice will be in vain... if that edifice is no longer habitable or if, renovated by others, it is nothing but a monument to the past, still worthy of respect and admiration but now only a witness to an age gone forever".[6]

An essential role in this new perspective, therefore, is to be played by history as science, which Loisy too advocated though not as an abstract or separate intellectual undertaking but as a decisive instrument to engender for the Church a new life. He was especially struck by the "incomplete yet enormous work already accomplished by Protestant and rationalist exegesis".[7] Science possesses a method of its own which does not differ substantially from that of historical disciplines,[8] and religious texts are not to be considered any differently but "according to the rules which are now applied to all human texts, taking into account the movement

---

[3]   "This uneasiness has grown over the last century with the advancement of our knowledge of the universe and of the ancient world. Scientific progress sheds a new light on the problem of God. The progress of history sheds new light on the problem of Christ and of the Church" (cf. PL, pp. XXIV-XXV).

[4]   PL, p. XXXV.

[5]   PL, p. 155.

[6]   PL, pp. 48-49.

[7]   PL, p. XVI.

[8]   "In historical investigation hypothesis plays the same role that it does in rigorous scientific research. The most valid hypothesis is the one that best takes account of the known facts and is best suited to them. A hypothesis which does not hold with respect to the facts is condemned, and not even discussed" (PL, pp. 35-36).

of contemporary thought within philosophy".[9] However, there is a specific limit to science and to history: they cannot bring us to the ultimate truth or the essence of things, they remain in a superficial or relative dimension, seeking that truth in the order of phenomena, i.e. in their sequentiality and in the causal link that orders their place in the world. In pursuing "the principle of divine truth concealed behind the formulas and the ancient conceptions",[10] we realize that even the teaching of Jesus is brought to us in the historical and human context of His coming and its announcement needs the symbols of mystery to reach us.[11]

Loisy needed this typical dualism to defend himself from his critics, in particular from ecclesiastical censorship. In relation to his previous work and to the theses contained in *The Gospel and the Church*, he repeatedly claimed that he had remained in the realm of science and had concerned himself only with history; the absolute, the truth or the fundamental principles of Christianity were not addressed in his work. This attitude, already present in his letters to Blondel,[12] is further clarified in the second "petit livre": "The aim of the book was not to demonstrate the divine truth of the Gospel or of the Church since history alone was not proof of this truth, which is not fully visible on the surface of things (which is what is offered to critical investigation) but is found above all in their intimate recesses and in the action of the Gospel on souls".[13] Loisy wavered between declaring truth to be inconceivable or impossible for humanity and attributing the knowledge of truth to theology, faith and inward experience,

---

[9]   PL, p. XXVIII. Cf. PL, p. 31: "... according to the rules which are suited to the study of all ancient texts", p. 57: "... it is inconceivable that the critical method applied to the Scriptures should differ from the one employed for other documents of antiquity", p. 64: "The assessment of ancient testimonies and the analysis of books are within the province of criticism, governed by laws which are the same for everyone".

[10]   PL, p. XXVIII.

[11]   "The representation of essential truths, limited as it is by symbols which stand for them only by analogy, without explaining them, can only be relative and imperfect, given the conditions of religious knowledge even in revelation which does not change the character of the human spirit, nor the forms of its action. In this connection does not St. Paul use the words mirror and enigma?" (PL, pp. 142-43. Cf. also PL, pp. 188-92, 198-99).

[12]   "Although there is no *separate history* in the absolute sense of your formula, it is true however that one may remain in the realm of facts placing there conclusions that, though not touching the essence of things, retain their importance" (a letter dated February 11, 1903, cf. CCM, p. 84).

[13]   PL, p. XXVII.

rigorously excluding science. On the other hand, whatever partakes of *reality* is only what pertains to the causal link within the world; truth, mystery and God, as such, run the risk of appearing unreal or fantastic because they do not belong to the scientific framework wherein the sense of all reality is decided.[14]

Yet the great respect for theology and for the tradition of the Church that this parallelism calls for is only illusory or feigned; they are in fact disregarded, i.e. declared as extrascientific, precisely by being extolled. Science deals with phenomena, faith instead deals with "intimate and profound truth",[15] although this does not constitute an advantage for faith which finds itself in the unauthentic sphere of the abstract, the unexpected and the fantastic. If religious truth is so elevated, unattainable or inexpressible, historical truth, controllable and accessible, is the only one within man's reach.[16] The life of faith or dogmatic tradition is not a valid element for the interpretation of the objective meaning of the texts. It must be found in another way, namely, through scientific research and eventually be directed to the elucidation or delimitation of religious experience.[17] This results in a significant reduction of the authority of the Church, which Loisy does not acknowledge as having a relatively independent historical memory of its own or the capacity to fix or express the events of its foundation. The Church might have authority if the Resurrection, on which it claims to be founded, were a historically determinable fact (but we know that this is impossible); on the other hand we cannot accept that fact solely

---

14   "History can only grasp phenomena, the order in which they occur and the interrelations among them; it perceives the manifestation of ideas and their evolution, but it does not reach the essence of things" (PL, pp. 9-10). Loisy compares the historian with the physicist in the sense that all they can grasp is a world of appearances; God "is not a personage of history", nor is He "an element of the physical world" (PL, p. 10). On the other hand, revelation takes place in humanity, according to its conditions of existence, and history does not grasp its profound truth: "The natural representation of things as they appear to the observer is perfectly compatible with their supernatural explanation. However this explanation is not the province of history" (PL, pp. 11-12).

15   PL, pp. 115-116.

16   "His method may be open to debate, but just as he did not, in any case, have the right to lie, it was his critics' duty to examine the true state of the questions. All the rest was nothing but groundless reasoning, superfluous rhetoric, sterile clamour" (PL, p. 13).

17   "Faith can be illumined by history, but history cannot be founded on faith" (PL, p. 14).

on the basis of the Church's authority. "It would be a contradiction to assume that an ecclesiastical definition can make a fact of the human order, which is not otherwise demonstrable, historically certain".[18]

A further determining element of the conflict seems to stem from the positivist preference for facts and distrust of ideas, especially when these ideas assume the meaning of a vast metaphysical construction. Yet if we argue — as Loisy often does — that historical research is concerned with facts and with the dogmatic definition of meanings, we do not arrive, as we may have hoped, at a precise criterion of distinction or of reciprocal delimitation. The sense of an event is also determined by the historical circumstances which produced it and, at any rate, there is a long tradition, within the framework of dogmatic thought, of converting ideas or beliefs that the historian might acknowledge only as such into facts. The facts that theology has in mind are too maleable, being bent to accomodate the exigencies of theory. Theology has turned Christ into a "divine automaton" who follows a "prearranged program", a "determinism" or a "mere game" in which the Apostles also take part, but this is "doctrine, not history".[19]

Yet there remains the possibility of assuming that history too attributes a sense to events, and that faith believes the factual and real character of its own dogmatic constructions: indeed it is against this false history, namely, sacred history, that Loisy's criticism is levelled, obviously to reassert the independence of biblical science from theology and apologetics.

Loisy believed (did he really?) that historical research would not disrupt the autonomous development of doctrine because it "tended to point out and represent facts which are in no way in contradiction with dogmas, precisely because they are facts, while dogmas are ideas representative of a faith that does not have as its object that which man can know, but the inexplicable of the divine".[20] However, he did not ask himself what a historical fact is, to what methodological conditions it should be

---

[18] PL, p. 14. Cf. PL, p. 11: "This history, even in the Gospel, is human history since it takes place in humanity. Jesus entered the history of men as a man, not as God".

[19] PL, pp. 18-19. Cf. PL, p. 42: "The task of the critic is to discuss biblical testimony, to examine its true importance, to distinguish between what are real facts and what is interpretation of faith, between what is primitive tradition and what is later tradition, to use each element according to its nature: the facts for historiography and traditional interpretation for the history of religious faith".

[20] PL, p. 51.

referred, or if one or more communities of reference, for instance scientific, prescientific or extrascientific, are at stake: some dogmas seem to establish facts, perhaps not in the sense that historical science would, but they are not mere ideas. On the other hand, history is also the "history of religious faith", that is, the history of beliefs that have real import for the community in which they originated, but which the historian methodically forbids himself to believe. That dogmatics is concerned merely with ideas is therefore true mainly for the scientific community, which does not attach any real significance to those propositions. The historicist imperialism noted earlier in Loisy resurfaces here from this dualism: Loisy advocated a general distrust as to the correspondence or fidelity of dogmatic sense to the historical sense of texts, dwelling on the imaginative speculative work of the "metaphysicians of dogma".[21] Between biblical and ecclesiastical testimony there is a one-way link of foundation, in no way reversible, and, since biblical testimony is fixed by science, it is the dogmatic elaboration, the decision of faith, that inevitably proves to be secondary: "the duty to regard the Bible as an authorized source of faith and as God's testimony of Himself does not logically precede but follows the historical consideration".[22]

This makes it much easier to comprehend what Loisy means when he states, within the framework of rigorous historical research, that the Church is the continuing Gospel and that there is a relation of necessary affiliation, of inevitable consequence between the two terms: it is not the "divine truth" of the Gospel and of the Church that is being referred to, but the connection of phenomena. Only in this way can the confutation of Harnack's primitivism take on a scientific meaning. However, Loisy does not reach a decision in this regard, wavering between two distinctly incompatible hypotheses: the continuist, evolutionary one whereby the essence of Christianity is that given through the entire development of the Catholic Church, and the "primitivist" one, like Harnack's, which emphasizes a primitive stratum of Christianity, recently highlighted by historical investigation, as opposed to subsequent constructions. As to the former, similar expressions may be found in the letters to Blondel dated February 1903 and in *Autour d'un petit livre* published in October. "My book

---

[21] PL, p. 51.
[22] PL, pp. 57-58. Immediately afterwards Loisy contradicts himself in his delineation of the "Catholic critic", faithful to the interpretation of the Church, "the collective and permanent consciousness of living Christianity" (PL, pp. 58-59).

contains only one thesis: the Church is the continuing Gospel; Christian development is not external or extraneous to the Gospel. This can be proven through a serious consideration of history, setting aside the divinity of the Gospel and that of the Church". Or again: "According to the historian, the Church proceeds from, but is not formally in the Gospel of Jesus. It was derived from the Gospel, from an inevitable evolution the conditions of which can be verified... Thus the Church was not only the inevitable consequence but the legitimate consequence of the Gospel. The aim of the book was not to demonstrate the divine truth of the Gospel and of the Church...".[23] The theorem that Loisy was attempting to demonstrate is that, on the plane of phenomena, the connections are such that they refute Harnack's search for an original nucleus, compared to which all that follows is presumably falsified or deviated. These connections, however, are necessary for an organic growth against a background of a general evolutionary philosophy. The subsequent developments, e.g. the present teachings of the Church, must not be taken as the result of an explication or logical deduction of principles contained in the Scriptures; in this respect everything has changed and will never cease to do so. But Christian doctrine remains the same if, through irriducible historical forms provided with autonomous substance, it is intended as a life that develops. "Asking the historian to find all of the present doctrine of the Church in biblical texts is like asking him to see in an acorn the roots, trunk and branches of a secular oak".[24] Thus, the confutation of Harnack remains insufficient because a "vital bond" cannot link historical facts unless this is effected through the debatable options of the philosophy of history.

On the other hand, Loisy's scientific intentions develop in another direction, which is much closer to the overall meaning of Harnack's position, that is, within the framework of his Christology. Loisy rejected Abbot Wehrlé's objections in this connection by asserting that he was an historian and not a theologian, and for this reason he did not possess a Christology.[25] But the distinction between a Christ of history and a Christ of faith, pursued from various angles and with remarkable insight, ended in a

---

[23] Cf. CCM, pp. 84-85 (letter dated February 11) and PL, pp. XXVI-XXVII.

[24] PL, pp. 65-66.

[25] "You are much better informed about my 'Christology' than I. The first two chapters deal with only what appears to the historian, therefore, there is no Christology. My Christology is that of the Church; I must add, however, that I believe this Christology to be susceptible of explanation" (cf. CCM, pp. 70-72).

new delineation of the figure of the Saviour according to the needs of "scientific faith", which Loisy argued were bound to impose themselves also within the Catholic Church. He applied different criteria to the selection and distribution of traditional materials. First of all, he drew a distinction between prevalently historical texts (which relate facts) and theoretical or doctrinal texts (which relate ideas) in the Scriptures and then argued that only the former (which are evidently also the most ancient ones) are historically relevant. He saw a vital (and not purely logical) development from the former to the latter, and for this reason it would be a radical mistake to project back into a relatively poor historical reality dogmatic constructions that developed much later, or to take as facts the images and symbols which try to express a complex conceptual situation. "I did not say that one must go back to the origin of Christian development to find the definitive and adequate expression of revealed truth. I confuted Harnack because this is what he demands. But determining the historical physiognomy of Christ is one thing, and defining and judging it from the point of view of faith is another... You simply do away with the Gospels as historical texts and you do not realize that, like other theologians, you want to oblige me to find in those texts what is not there, and force me to torture the Synoptics to make them say what is in John", he wrote to Blondel on February 22, 1903.[26] In Loisy's view, the Gospel of John is in effect and in every respect "unhistorical", therefore unusable; John's ideas do not contradict the facts in the Synoptics except in that they are ideas and as such extraneous to the historical dimension of the Gospels. To be sure, this Gospel also speaks to us of the extreme power contained in the kernel, that is, in Christ's work, "but the initial and concrete form of this work cannot be determined except through the texts that directly reflect the teaching and action of the Saviour". Otherwise, warned Loisy, arousing traditional dogmatic exigencies, we will lose all foundation in reality and be forced to admit that we know nothing about the historical event.[27]

At the basis of this reasoning is still a rather uncertain notion of history and of historical fact. To traditionalists, sacred history is not subject to the common criteria of the new historical science and so, basically, it coincides with doctrine or with dogma, although for Loisy this is only a false history to be replaced by the true history of scientific research. How could theologians be made to understand that fundamental dogmas such as the Immaculate Conception or the Resurrection, which they take to be

---

26   CCM, p. 97.
27   CCM, p. 98. Cf. PL, pp. 85 ff.

facts and treat accordingly, escape the reality of history and historical knowledge? According to Loisy, theology materialized symbolic representations into a factual and real form which cannot withstand rigorous investigation. In other words, it ascribed the modern and scientific sense of historicity to what was viewed as history in the doctrinal and ecclesiastical realm.[28] And the precise reason for which the quality of historical event cannot be attributed to the Resurrection is not, as Abbot Gayraud contended, the absence of contact with the senses. Rather, it is the absence of fundamental theoretical principles of the modern scientific method: understanding a phenomenon means placing it in the possible and observable connections within this world; what does not belong to this world is the object neither of science nor of history.[29]

The first evangelical narratives were therefore transformed into an increasingly idealized form which ended up concealing the facts: "... the glory of the risen Christ influences the memory of His earthly life in such a way as to adapt it to the conditions of the immortal Christ". The apostles were not looking for the exactness of historical facts, but were concerned with the conversion of their listeners; thus, "... in relating the Gospel, they interpreted it". In this way the "first Christological speculations" originated and were later developed in the Fourth Gospel.[30] According to Loisy, the prescience, the rationality and the almost "automatic" behavior of John's Christ are not realistic: they reflect a conception of the sacred text in which

---

[28] Father M.J. Lagrange, director of the Bible School of Jerusalem, which he founded in 1890, wrote the following about Loisy's views in 1903: "In a way it can be said that the Incarnation is not a historical fact, nor is the Resurrection of Jesus Christ in that He is constituted in His glory; at any rate, it is certain that history is incapable of ascertaining the divinity of Christ. History can establish the facts of His life that may serve as the basis of the act of faith" ("Jésus et la critique des Evangiles", *Bulletin de Litt. ecclésiastique*, December 1903 - January 1904, pp. 3-26; in the appendix to the third edition of *La méthode historique* [Paris: Lecoffre, 1904] pp. 221-59. Cf. M.J. Lagrange, *La méthode historique. La critique biblique et l'Eglise* [Paris: Ed. du Cerf, 1966] p. 185). Lagrange returned to the subject many years later to comment on the publication of Loisy's *Memoirs* (*M. Loisy et le modernisme* [Paris: Les Ed. du Cerf, 1932]).

[29] Abbot Gayraud had contested Loisy in various articles published in *L'Univers* from October to November 1903: "On what grounds does Loisy claim that the risen Christ *could* not be the object of sensible experience and that the entry of a body into immortal life must *always and necessarily* be unobservable?...In this regard the evangelical narratives demonstrate the opposite" (cf. E. Poulat, HDC, pp. 192-93, note 8).

[30] PL, pp. 83-85.

facts are always signs or symbols and as such do not count. Just as Christ is the temporal manifestation and incarnation of God, also the Gospel according to John is an incarnation, a symbolic and material translation of a profound meaning or of an "invisible truth": "And so the Gospel, like Christ, is made of divine spirit beneath a human exterior, and it is necessary to seek the inner spirit in which to believe. It may be said that Christ is a personal and divine allegory, and the Gospel is the Word Incarnate".[31]

As for the separation of the historical element from the theological element in the figure of the Saviour, one should not only refer solely to the Synoptics, leaving the Fourth Gospel to the history of Christian beliefs, but also criticize a whole set of notions which were unjustifiably added to the historical event. "The divinity of Jesus is not an element of evangelical history the reality of which can be verified critically, but it is the definition of the relation between Christ and God, namely, a belief the origin and development of which the historian can only trace". This is a theological statement subsequent to the historical reality of the Synoptics; in other words, it is a doctrine "resulting from theological speculation" which does not belong to the "personal teaching of the Saviour".[32] In a way it is not surprising that theology has asserted the divinity of Christ, since theology does not have to define historically the preaching or the consciousness of the Saviour but what Jesus has meant to Christian consciousness; between the consciousness of Jesus as it appears to history and the "metaphysical definitions" of the Councils "there is the same difference as the one between reality and the abstract".[33] Even the dogma of the hypostatic union, of the association between the two natures, "does not change the conditions of the historical testimony to the life, works and teachings of Jesus. The

---

[31]   Cf. PL, pp. 91-97. In John we presumably find for the first time a speculative theology in which miraculous events are seen as the expression or proof of the divinity of Jesus: "Given that His teaching has as its sole aim the divinity of His person and of His mission, he works miracles only to substantiate what He teaches, to 'manifest His glory', as is said of the miracle of the Wedding Feast. Such miracles are at once proofs of His omnipotence and symbols from which His spiritual work transpires" (PL, p.92).

[32]   PL, pp. 130-31. However at the same time Loisy emphasizes the element of continuity: "There are no divisions between the event and its interpretation, which is not a fiction foreign to the event. Reciprocally, the evangelical event, if understood correctly, is not against theological interpretation, nor does it weaken or annul it". (PL, pp. 135-36).

[33]   PL, pp. 136-37. What occurs instead is that dogma, which is a "doctrinal construction" is understood by theologians as "psychological reality" in the consciousness of Christ, in substitution of real psychological reality, which, is

historian, it must be reiterated, judges this dogma to be a theoretical definition elaborated in the course of the early Christian age, not a verifiable reality demonstrated directly by historical documents".[34] The divine institution of the Church and of the sacraments too is an "object of faith, not a historically demonstratable fact". Besides, Loisy argues, this divine institution has meaning if Christ is God, but the divinity of Christ is in turn an element of faith, attested by the Church: the divine character of Christ and of the Church refer back to each other.[35] The same can be said for the Resurrection in that the divine institution of the Church is an act of the risen Christ: "... to the historian who is content with considering facts which can be observed, the Church was founded on the faith in Christ; from the point of view of faith, it was instituted by Christ Himself".[36] If we accept that in the New Tesatament the glorified Christ alone founds the Church and the sacraments, "it follows that both the institution of the Church and of the sacraments and the glorification of Christ are the object of faith, not of historical proof".[37]

Loisy, however, also intended to demythologize the theological-metaphysical formulas of Catholic tradition: not simply by dismissing them as being unacceptable or unintelligible to modern culture, but by attempting to translate or decode them so that they could be brought back to the fundamental meaning, humanistic and progressivist, of his religious conceptions. Whatever theology attributed to the risen Christ, history attributed to the community of believers. For instance, if the institution of the sacrament of Baptism can be traced to a few words of Christ glorified,[38] we could think that "the Gospel attests that the rite originated in the apostolic community. The apparition described by Matthew is like a concise summary of the traditions linked to the Resurrection, and to the historian the words of Christ express a living sentiment of Christian consciousness".[39] In other words, to speak of the risen Christ could be an

---

      determinable only by history, if it is determinable at all (cf. PL, p. 149).

[34] PL, p. 147.

[35] PL, pp. 161-62.

[36] PL, p. 172. Cf. also PL, p. 74: "Christ's wishes regarding the Church can be determined only by the Church and for those who have recognized Christ in the Church".

[37] PL, p. 227.

[38] "Go then and teach all nations, baptizing them in the name of the Father and of the Son and of the Holy Spirit" (*Matthew* 28:19).

[39] PL, p. 229. Many other examples may be cited, cf. PL, p. 231, in which the narratives of the fourth Gospel, precisely because they could be the "words of

archaic or outdated way of speaking about the community, of the Church. It is in this way that Loisy expressed the sociological-positivist (durkheimian) element of his background, as well as the orientation that later was to lead him towards a religion of humanity.[40]

Loisy's position in this second stage seems to converge with Harnack's. The distinction between the Synoptics and the Fourth Gospel seems to reflect the distinction between biblical history and theological doctrine, and to Loisy John becomes the first "metaphysician of dogma" who does not really narrate the life of Christ. They therefore both reject subsequent "speculations": Harnack does so in order to recover the moral foundation (the "Gospel of Jesus", namely, Christ's original preaching as opposed to the "Gospel about Jesus" of the early communities), while Loisy seeks to recover the historical foundation and, perhaps, the human character of the Saviour.[41] For the "Gospel of Jesus" (or from the historical point of view as regards Loisy) there is no such thing as sacraments, the divinity of Christ or the Resurrection, in short, all that Harnack called the "Gospel about Jesus", namely, theological or metaphysical Christology. Thus even Loisy, paradoxically, was concerned with identifying an original stratum, the only true one in the view of historical science, a discipline that they both had chosen as the instrument for attaining a new Christian life.

---

the glorious Christ anticipated during His earthly life", are interpreted by the historian as "the expression of Christian sentiment, a testimony of Christian faith"; PL, pp. 233-34, while for the historian the institution of the sacraments does not derive from Christ but from the community; PL, pp. 244-45, 252, for the distinction between the attitude of the historian (whose object is only "the exteriority" or the "work of Christian consciousness") and the attitude of faith: "It is easy to notice (in the definitions of the Council of Trent) the confusion between historical criteria, criteria of faith and criteria of theological speculation. Why should this confusion continue, and why should it be imposed on the historian who, after having perceived it, cannot accept it?" (PL, p. 254).

[40] Cf. Appendix.

[41] It is remarkable that Harnack's distinction between the "Gospel of Jesus" and the "Gospel about Jesus" is echoed in Loisy's words referring to the theological elaboration of the early Christian age: "How could it have been useless, given that he did not wish to define historically the teaching of Jesus, but what Jesus meant to Christian consciousness?" (PL, p. 136).

VI

Blondel: the Return to Tradition

To simplify the situation in the extreme, one might say that while Loisy wished to subordinate theology to history, Blondel wished to do the exact opposite. In the letters he sent to Loisy in February 1903 Blondel already seemed concerned about what he called the "chimerical neutrality" of historical science and about its claims to independence, which meant that the modes or forms of necessary collaboration with other disciplines were obscured.[1] He had already expressed his reservations about the historical method in the *Lettre* of 1896,[2] and *Histoire et dogme* may be considered an expansion and continuation of this: in historicist apologetics, intended as programmatically aphilosophical and atheological, the living relation with God, His continuing presence in man's life (and in the Church's), is overshadowed.[3] History considers remote or past facts superficially, but reality proper, the "essence of things" which Loisy the historian methodically forbids himself to consider,[4] is the Incarnation: the

---

[1] Cf. CCM, pp. 77, 101 (the letters dated February 6 and 27). Cf. R. Aubert, "La position de Loisy au moment de sa controverse avec M. Blondel", in *Journées d'études, 9-10 novembre 1974, Blondel-Bergson-Maritain-Loisy* (Louvain: Ed. Peeters, 1977) pp. 75-90.

[2] "Lettre sur les exigences de la pensée contemporaine en matière d'apologétique", in *Les premiers écrits de M. Blondel* (Paris: PUF, 1956) (henceforth referred to as PE) pp. 10-13. Cf. "Cristianesimo e filosofia nella 'Lettera' del 1896", an introductory essay on M. Blondel, *Lettera sull'apologetica*, ed. G. Forni (Brescia: Queriniana, 1990).

[3] In his objections to Loisy, Blondel remarked that "the claim to separate systematically the historical point of view, in this matter, from all that is metaphysical or theological appears untenable to me... this method could only lead to the omission or suppression of the supernatural" (Blondel to Bremond, January 4, 1903, cf. CCM, p. 52)

[4] Cf. PL, pp. 9-12 and the letter to Blondel dated February 11, 1903 (CCM, p. 84).

presence of Christ in our lives and in history, which continues to the end of time and makes any "purely historical" consideration of humanity grossly inadequate. This presence is at the basis of individuals joining together to form a community or a church, and therefore it is also at the basis of the subsequesnt testimony that the Christian community offers of the founding events of the past, which cannot be reduced to historical certification. It cannot be said, as Loisy does, that events established empirically (through the means commonly available to science) are at the basis of the life of the Church, for the Church too has a memory of its own and it legitimately refers to historical events.

The hermeneutical question raised by Blondel has a meaning which extends beyond the religious sphere. First of all, it has an anti-intellectualist meaning because it is the living relationship between individuals engaged in a common effort that determines a certain past. Loisy and Blondel are both critical, though in different ways, of the Protestant tendency towards individual scientific research (instead of towards praxis, or collective life) as the source of fundamental truths. Moreover Blondel has no intention of constructing a specific hermeneutics for theology; the same is true of Loisy, but for very different reasons. If Loisy holds historicist methodology to be sufficient also for religious issues,[5] Blondel on the contrary does not believe this method to be sufficient or adequate, not even for human problems in general. The whole of human existence is wrapped in mystery (or better, it is rooted in the Christological mystery of its origin and its goal); therefore superficial historical investigation, purported as absolute, would result in diverting attention from the substance of the problem. A realistic Christology cannot therefore have recourse to biblical science alone; it requires extrahistorical means, that is, reference to the tradition of the Church and the experience of faith. Loisy's Christology essentially stems from his refusal to deal with the "essence of things"; but the phenomenistic Christ of history is only one aspect of the "total" Christ (of faith, of the Church, of theological and philosophic reflection) who is at the foundation of all reality.

Blondel, however, did not intend to reject historical factuality, the necessity of which he had already attempted to show in the *Lettre*.[6] The

---

[5]　Cf. PL, pp. XXVIII, 31, 35-36, 57, 64.

[6]　"And so after having discarded all questions of fact or of person in order to define the notion of supernatural, in the end we would be led... to rekindle the need for the concrete reality of the Word in its most precise form, to insert solely at this point historical apologetics and to justify man's need to study, acknowledge and reenact one event among other events, the divine event of Christianity" (PE, pp. 90-91).

problem lies elsewhere: whether Christ (as man) is confined within the bounds of factuality to the point of losing the awareness of His divine nature and of His work or whether He retains this awareness. According to Blondel, the chief meaning of the "lowering" of Christ is not one of redemption (to take upon Himself the sins of the world), but a cosmic, primitive meaning in that it reinforces the universe's response to its Creator: "... if things are active and truly real, if they exist in their objective appearance, in short, if they are, it is because the divine eye sees them through the eye of the creature, not so much because it creates them as because they are created and their author himself becomes passive with respect to their action".[7] In the *Lettre* he had already expounded two Christological theses: one that, given the Crucifixion and the Redemption, there is no other reason for the Incarnation of the Word than the sins of man; the other that "the original plan of Creation included the mystery of God as Man", which he clearly preferred.[8] It seemed to him at this point that Loisy was stressing the human side of Christ, subjecting Him to historical circumstances and making Him unaware of the universal import of His work; thus Christological questions urge him towards a more general reflection on the historical method.[9]

Histoire et dogme (1904) was no doubt a confutation of Loisy, although Blondel decidedly denied that this was the meaning of his work. Rather, the object of his research was "abstract theses in their schematic form", and he even cited passages from Loisy which seemed to contradict

---

[7] M. Blondel, *L'Action* (1893) (Paris: PUF, 1974) p. 459. Cf. also *Carnets intimes*, vol. I: 1883-1894 (Paris: Ed. du Cerf, 1961) pp. 113-14: "The Mediator repeats the act of Creation: everything was made by Him; nothing would exist without Him; without Him all that was made would be nothing, that is, without His presence in His work, without His glance, without His humanity. One is what one knows and loves. Nothing can be unless it is known and loved by God; it is through the action of man that the Word became the world, *Verbum caro factum est*".

[8] PE, p. 89. Cf. A. Boland, *La crise moderniste hier et aujourd'hui* (Paris: Beauchesne, 1980) chapter IV: "Du Christ à la christologie", pp. 91-117; X. Tilliette, "M. Blondel et la controverse christologique", in *Le modernisme* (Paris: Beauchesne, 1980) pp. 129-160; G.Forni, "Blondel e la controversia cristologica", in *Annali di storia dell'esegesi*, 11/1 (1994), pp. 229-265.

[9] Cf. the letter to Wehrlé dated December 10, 1902 (CCM, p. 49). Also M. Nédoncelle, "Les rapports de l'histoire et du dogme d'après Blondel", II. "La conscience du Christ", in *Journées d'études*, cit., pp. 99-104.

his radical historicism.[10] On the other hand it seemed that the two scholars agreed on certain issues such as Newman's notion of development. "On many points", Blondel remarked after having read *L'Evangile e l'Eglise*, "I found nothing but triteness, ideas which form the habitual atmosphere of my thought, such as the notion of organic growth, the sentiment of those transformations which alter the letter without changing the spirit... the conviction of the vital needs which instinctively inspired the Church to be at every moment of its history what it had to be in order to live".[11] Yet Blondel mistrusted a certain phenomenalism or determinism in Loisy that considered historical necessity as an exterior connection, and he turned to the inner forces that guide the process; not a pantheistic or mechanical development, but a *Christian* development in the way that "a seed adapts to everything and organically assimilates the most varied nutriments.[12] In other words, while scientific explanation is acknowledged, it remains confined "within the limits of a closed determinism that touches upon nothing but exterior pressures or intersecting influences (evolution)", and must thus open itself "to an extrascientific explantion, organic and vital, which corresponds to a continuous creation starting from a seed which assimilates its nutriments (development)".[13] This solution appeared all the

---

[10] Cf. PE, p. 193: "What I am criticizing is the thesis advancing the compartmentalization of history and dogma and the immeasurability of statements of faith and truth resulting from facts; that is all the more reason for the thesis of the opposition between the former and the latter and of the double-entry book-keeping of consciousness".

[11] A. Bremond, January 4, 1903 (CCM, p. 52). Loisy had already written "Le développement chrétien d'après le card. Newman" (*Revue du clergé français*, December 1, 1898, pp. 5-20), an article hailed as "decidedly remarkable" and "very intelligent" also by J. Guitton (cf. *La philosophie de Newman. Essai sur l'idée de Développement* [Paris: Boinvin, 1933] pp. 122 and 224). For a comprehensive view of the question, see P. Gauthier, *Newman et Blondel. Tradition et développement du dogme* (Paris: Ed. du Cerf, 1988) chapter X: "Blondel et Loisy", pp. 209-236.

[12] Cf. the letter to Loisy dated February 6, 1903 (CCM, p. 74).

[13] C. Théobald, "L'entrée de l'histoire dans l'univers religieux et théologique au moment de la 'crise moderniste'", in J. Greisch, K. Neufeld, C. Théobald, *La crise contemporaine. Du modernisme à la crise des herméneutiques*, cit., p. 55 (for the quotation from *Histoire et Dogme*, cf. PE. p. 190). Cf. H. Gouhier, "Tradition et développement à l'époque du modernisme", in *Ermeneutica e tradizione*, edited by E. Castelli (Padova: Cedam, 1963) p. 91: "Where Loisy says: evolution *or* development, Blondel says: evolution *and* development. The term which recalls Spencer is used to denote intelligible continuity and therefore scientific explanation through determinism. The term which recalls Newman, is ascribed to spiritual continuity and therefore to a realist explanation in which biological analogies will prevail".

more necessary to Blondel insofar as the continuum of the positivist historian (*from* the Gospel *to* the Church) could indeed not be founded merely on empirical research but required a "guiding idea", an "initial orientation", an "original impulse", in short, philosophical or theological options.[14]

One begins to understand, then, in what sense historical research must be linked to other disciplines yet retain a subordinate role. "The technical and critical nature of history, in a precise, scientific sense, is not real history, a substitute for humanity's concrete experience of life, historical truth in its entirety. Between these two histories, one a science and the other life, one proceeding from a phenomenological method and one tending to represent a substantial reality, there is an enormous gap to fill".[15] In other words, it seems that within the framework of modernity, and following the rise of the new historical sciences, a division arose between two types of history: history as science (which takes no account of the mediation of faith or of the Church, as in Loisy) and history as life, or history as reality (which accepts this mediation). Blondel is thus faced with the problem of a "Catholic exegesis" that is not merely science, but a science bound up with the life of the Church — one that attributes a positive, indispensable role to historical-critical research, and avoids the shortcomings of *extrinsicism* ("those who tend to act as if history depended entirely on dogma"), but integrates its results with the insights from the theological disciplines so as to avoid the pitfall of *historicism* ("those who act as if dogma derived exclusively from history and subordinated itself to it").[16] Yet one problem remains: if the break which has been discussed can be traced to a separation between *facts* and *ideas*, as some of Blondel's assertions seem to suggest, then there could be a relation of reciprocity, of circularity between history and dogma: the one orients the other, facts elicit beliefs and these organize empirical research ("the passage from historical data to faith, which is something more than what they represent for the mere witness — the passage from faith to truly objective assertions and to realities which constitute a Sacred History at the core of common history and embodying ideas in facts").[17] However, if the distinction between the two histories cannot be traced to the distinction between facts and ideas (and it cannot, for scientific research too makes use of hypotheses, that is,

---

[14]   Cf. the letter to Loisy of February 6, 1903 (CCM, p. 74).
[15]   PE, p. 170.
[16]   PE, pp. 152-53.
[17]   PE, p. 152.

of its own conceptual framework, and theology, the doctrine of faith, makes reference to historical events), it would be difficult to justify a metaphysical or *parallel* theological historicity as opposed to common historiography.[18]

At first Blondel approaches his argument by presenting a dualism whose meaning is doubtful. We are to look for a relation (a reconciliation, a synthesis) between history and dogma — in other words, between "critical method" and the "necessary authority of doctrinal formulas", "Christian facts" and "Christian beliefs", "facts" and "ideas".[19] This terminology must be examined very carefully: two authorities (corresponding to two communities) are at stake, the authority of science and that of faith. Also at stake are the two areas wherein each community works out and propounds its thought, "facts" and "ideas" (of course, the issue is further complicated if one thinks, as is the case, that the scientific community has its ideas and the religious community its facts). Moreover, the historical facts espoused by science are not sufficient to produce the system of Christian belief, nor is this system sufficient to produce historical facts,[20] although the dogmatic system produces factual convictions which run parallel to those of science — a "historical reality", a "Sacred History". The question is posed clearly enough, but there is a risk of using the notions of fact and historical reality in a way that may be difficult to justify.

---

[18] Cf. Abbot Venard's criticism: "The synoptic gospels have transmitted only incomplete memories, it is true... they are however the most faithful echo of the apostolic memories: would it not be a risk to wish to correct them and to fill the gaps with inferences based on statements of faith? In a way would it not amount to adopting the false method which Blondel criticized as *extrinsicism* based on the belief that historical reality can be deduced from the formulas of dogma?" (L. Venard, "La valeur historique du dogme", *Bulletin de Litt. ecclésiastique*, VI, November-December 1904, p. 355. Cited by R. Virgoulay, *Blondel et le modernisme. La philosophie de l'action et les sciences religieuses, 1896-1913* [Paris: Ed. du Cerf, 1980] p. 383).

[19] Cf. PE, pp. 150-53. Other expressions used on page 152 are: "facts" and "beliefs" (l. 6), "historical facts" and "Catholic faith" (ll. 8-9), "Catholic faith" and "facts", "historical reality" (ll. 11-14), "crude facts" and "dogmatic ideas" (ll. 17-18), "historical data" and "faith" (l. 21), "faith" and "truly objective assertions", "reality" (ll. 23-24).

[20] Cf. PE, p. 152: "if it is true that historical facts are at the basis of the Catholic faith, they alone do not generate faith, nor are they sufficient to justify it completely; conversely, the Catholic faith and the authority of the Church which it entails ensure the facts and extract from them a doctrinal interpretation which in turn is imposed on the believer as a historical reality, but for reasons other than those of which the historian is the judge".

What do these terms mean once they have been removed from the epistemological context of the historical sciences? What are "Christian facts"[21] if we do not know upon what method, approach or community of reference they are based? Moreover, Blondel's exposition may appear misleading because the contrast is not between *facts* and *ideas*, but between different systems of reference that produce both "facts" and "ideas". In this respect, Blondel seems immediately to dehistoricize the Catholic faith, turning it into a system of beliefs, a speculative organism producing its own historical "events", although this would bring him too close to the extrinsicist tendency, which he himself refuses to admit.

Once the contrast is set up, Blondel considers its "incomplete and incompatible" solutions: the traditional, scholastic one (extrinsicism) and the modern, critical one (historicism). As I have already mentioned, *Histoire et dogme* is largely a polemic against Loisy, so that little attention is devoted to the first tendency. "Since neither facts nor ideas alone are enough for faith, to which, if any, does one turn for the element capable of effecting their synthesis? To know what history can and must give dogma, and what dogma can and must give history, it seems necessary to ask: on what common ground does this exchange between them occur, and how are the links between them established?".[22] Extrinsicism was meant to answer this kind of question, although in it the factual dimension, in the sense used in the modern historical sciences, is altogether missing. Every supposed "fact" is simply taken from theological doctrine, not to mention that extrinsicist theologians are not interested in historical reality as such but only in any miraculous traits, which are used to support dogmatic theses.[23] Blondel instead states that historicism is the "principal aim of this work".[24]

In Blondel's view the subordinate character of history is determined by the same reasons which make it the supreme science for Loisy. It cannot be said that history is "independent", or that "it is sufficient unto itself", nor that "it arrives at doctrinal conclusions of which it is ultimately the judge and which grasp the whole of reality". No, "it inevitably remains linked to further issues, to higher sciences which it can replace or supplement only through usurpation, setting itself up under the false name of a kind of total metaphysics, of universal vision or of a *Weltanschaung*".[25]

---

[21] Cf. PE, p. 152 (l. 1), p.163 (ll. 1-2), p. 186 (ll. 4, 11), p. 197 (l. 3).

[22] PE, pp. 153-54.

[23] PE, pp. 155-57.

[24] PE, p. 161.

[25] PE, p. 164.

This judgement depends on Blondel's phenomenistic conception of history that derives from Kant. Like Loisy, he admits that science does not arrive at the "essence of things"[26] and it is entirely constructed in the dimension of appearance, establishing the necessary connections. Yet this limit, which for Loisy constitutes the strong point of his discipline, to the philosopher means the inferiority and impotence of history in defining the profound reality, which is determined in the realm of metaphysics or theology. The historian grasps the external, not the internal, the *expression* or manifestation, not *life*: "By seeking to become first and foremost the eternal contemporary of past ages... the historian sets out through science to recover not real life, but the clearest expression, as far as possible, of this reality and the explanation of the determinism which — seemingly — has linked all the subsequent moments".[27] Blondel thus accepts determinism, but only as a rule of "external" history, as a law of phenomena; in the opposites of necessity-freedom, matter-spirit, external-internal, which he retains from the Kantian legacy, history is on the side of necessity and matter. Instead of refounding or reformulating the historical method, removing it from positivism if necessary, Blondel prefers to accept it in the form in which it is transmitted to him, because science never touches what is deepest in the human soul or what is truly human.[28]

At the same time, Blondel sought to overcome this split by means of the theme of *interpretation*, namely, the necessary, subjective conditioning of historical research, the inevitable grounding of purported scientific neutrality in moral, metaphysical and religious options: "... real history is made of human lives; and human life is metaphysics in progress".[29] In this

---

[26] Cf. PE, p. 166: "these sciences therefore differ less in the diversity of distinct objects, which they aid in making known in their ultimate reality, than in the diversity of methods and points of view open to a further problem which they contribute to defining, preparing and posing, rather than solving at the root".

[27] PE, p. 167.

[28] Although history advances on the plane of "observable manifestations" and fails to grasp the "interior workings" of humanity, it constructs "a coherent whole" (PE, p. 167); in other words, it is the product of modern science and it accepts (with full legitimacy) its determinist hypothesis. Cf. PE, p. 176 (ll. 6-12), p. 188, note 1.

[29] Cf. PE, p. 168: "One must never think it possible to grasp, with the sole aid of historical science, a fact, which is only a fact and is the whole fact: each link of the chain, like the chain itself, entails psychological and moral problems affected by the slightest action and testimony... Founding a historical science independent of any ideal concerns, presuming that the lower part of history

approach, the internal and the external (but also necessity and freedom, matter and spirit, along with the disciplines of which those terms are a synthetic expression, in particular science and philosophy) might be joined once again, paradoxically removing history from the scientific objectivism he had previously acknowledged.[30] Moreover the introduction of the contrast between history and reality, and history and science further complicates the matter because if history as science is phenomenistic or deterministic, the history of historians (a recurrent figure in the clash with Loisy and which shows a clear dependence on Loisy's approach), history as life (or reality) is a *new* figure indicating that ontological totality, that deep truth which heretofore had seemed to be the preserve of philosophy.[31] But who is to be the practitioner of such a history, and with what tools? In this new dualism, unlike in the previous one, the theme of interpretation is lost again, for instead of problematizing the historical method (in a sense which would be called hermeneutic or anti-positivist today) it is basically accepted as is in order to go beyond it or to duplicate it, though no longer in the direction of philosophy but towards a new "history".[32]

Let us try then to comprehend this methodologically indecipherable meaning of the new "history" advocated by Blondel. It can be treated from two points of view: the first is to bend the historical method to the exigencies of theology and of the Church, to limit its ambitions and possibilities through a total acceptance of traditional faith, though avoiding the simple rejection (extrinsicism) or condemnation of modern science. The second is

---

can, strictly speaking, be a positive ascertainment means allowing oneself to be dominated by predetermined opinions with the pretext of impossible neutrality... In the absence of an explicit philosophy, an unconscious philosophy usually develops. What one holds to be simple observations are often constructs". Also see PE, p. 175 (ll. 20-23).

[30] However scientific research is always considered "inferior" ("subalternes", PE, p. 169, l. 2).

[31] Cf. PE, pp. 169-70. Is a philosophical *history*, a theological *history* possible? For instance, what does it mean to speak of "assertions of the moral or theological order which were offered as an interpretation, a historical interpretation, of the facts" (PE, p. 170)?

[32] Later, in expounding the weaknesses of historicism (PE, pp. 172-73), Blondel again relies heavily on dualisms (phenomenon-noumenon, science-philosophy). Science, which at least provided us with one side or aspect of the truth, of the total being, can no longer provide anything; it is trapped in the dimension of an image or picture. If science (history) does provide something, however, it is not simply because it is *receptive* to other disciplines, but because it *subjects itself* to other disciplines, the sciences of being and truth.

the movement through which Blondel's explicit intentions end up problematizing the historical method on its own ground, leading it beyond the positivist configuration towards results that in current terminology could be called hermeneutical. The theme of interpretation arises because it first appears in Blondel's argument. Other themes, partially characterizing the new history, were to follow: what we might call the themes of historical *stratification* and of the *circle* of comprehension. "The critical historian must not in fact ask himself what he would have thought or done had he lived in Judea around the year 40 A.D. since he cannot avoid living in the twentieth century or taking into account both the darkness and the light that have accompanied the passing of the centuries". This is certainly a way of contesting any form of historiographic "primitivism", in other words, of rejecting (within a vision that can be only secular and scientific) the attempt to trace an original stratum independently of historical mediations or of traditions also shared by the historian. Yet Blondel goes on to say: "It is to the whole that judgement is directed. If the historian reaches apologetical conclusions, to him they will be the real and actual conditions of the adherence to real and actual Christianity". Therefore, whenever we try to move from the abstract to the concrete, "from expressive particulars to the whole", we are faced with a hermeneutic problem which can be dealt with as such. In other words, how the totality of the whole leads to the knowledge of its single aspects and viceversa. This historiographic primitivism is wanting precisely from the point of view of the historical method. But that is not all Blondel means. He does not thoroughly treat distinct levels of analysis or deal thematically with topics as his aim is the totality of a process *qua* the basis of historical understanding (a methodological problem) and, more deeply still, the Christological substance of reality and of the Church *qua* the origin and sense of all history (a metaphysical and theological issue). "The whole can be known only from the particular. The journey of the human spirit is an analysis between two syntheses: how can one prevent the first synthesis, divinatory and hypothetical, from influencing analysis, with the risk of predetermining the final synthesis?... metaphysical problems are never completely extraneous to the spirit of this journey, for they are antecedent, concomitant and successive to any positive research regarding man".[33]

---

[33]   Cf. PE, pp. 174-75. Also in the pages that follow Blondel fails to draw a clear distinction between historical stratification and Catholic tradition, between a hermeneutical issue and a metaphysical-religious one. This overlap is particularly noticeable in certain points: cf. PE, p. 177, ll. 15-17 ("To know the true Christ will we instead have the opportunity to make use of the

Of course, the hermeneutical or theological objection to historiographic primitivism was aimed at Harnack, and more directly at Loisy. It was easy for Blondel to show hermeneutically that Loisy's determinism also meant continuum, evolutionism and immanentism, that is, a metaphysics of history not necessarily demanded by a historical *method*.[34] Theologically, according to Blondel, Loisy was still bound to an abstract or unilateral position, "primitivist" in the sense that he did not consider the totality implied by historical research.

To be sure, Loisy had opposed the primitivism in Harnack, who propounded an original stratum, by showing the substantial continuity of Christianity through the centuries: there are historians who "have assumed that they could unite, together and indissolubly, free science and historical apologetics".[35] But this "free science" was to become an absolute to the point of subordinating or eliminating the position of faith and of the Church, so that "what was only positive history is presented as negative theology".[36] The two possible directions of Loisy's undertaking must both be rejected: for evolutionary continuity is fundamentally a falsification, in a naturalistic or immanentistic sense, of the full Christian truth (as it does not place the historical problem within the ever present issue of the life of Christ, of the

---

comprehensive effort of generations of believers and make the currents of life and thought accumulated in the course of nineteen centuries on the Gospel flow back to the source?"); in addition, on p. 181, ll. 11-15 with reference to the historian of Christianity who "if he continues his work of historical analysis and reconstruction using narratives and texts as his only materials, can it be said that he is faithful to his law, a law whereby considering the whole must precede the formulation of definitive conclusions?".

[34] According to Blondel, "... against the conclusions of those who are too quick in saying: that is what was, therefore, that is how it had to be, the following reservation is necessary: the natural continuity of history does not prove that history is enough to justify this development naturally. The more one attempts to *confine* the facts to their determinism, as if everything proceeded by itself, the more these explanations will appear inadequate". Loisy's stand is summarized as follows: "Despite all the causes of failure, the Catholic Church has survived over the centuries... furthermore, this continuity can and must be understood in terms of a logical development... of a progressive adjustment of Christian society to the upward movement of humanity" (PE, pp. 188-89). Cf. EE, pp. 152-53, and PL, pp. XXVI-XXVII.

[35] PE, p. 163. Cf. Loisy's letter to Blondel dated February 11, 1903: "It seems to me that few scholars have had the idea of a historical defence of religion. Now, this idea has been the folly of my life" (CCM, p. 82).

[36] PE, p. 171.

faith of His Church);[37] and the search for an original truth that excludes both this faith and the subsequent developments of Christianity is twice as disappointing because it lacks the basic totality, of faith and of history, in which all research should be rooted.[38] In the latter case the discontinuity could be accentuated and suspicions as to the fidelity of dogmatic development could be warranted (Blondel recalls Loisy's famous proposition "Jesus foretold the Kingdom, and it was the Church that came"[39] without citing the source), for example, by linking the historical figure of Jesus too closely to the Hebrew component (the notions of the Kingdom and of the Messiah), thereby severing it from the Christ of faith, that is, from the successive dogmatic evolution.[40]

Blondel wanted to re-establish the rights of ecclesiastical Tradition as the legitimate source of historical knowledge, although this would have required methodological and conceptual clarification of the new historicity and of its relation to "critical" history. For instance, what does "the History that Catholicism forces us to believe is not only the history that the historian can establish" mean if no indication is given to enable us to understand it or to construct it?[41] There are indications, albeit sketchy, and the last part

---

[37] "Thus when we are asked to establish that the Church is simply the continuation of the Gospel, this appealing and fecund thesis ... proves disappointing and chimerical from the point of view of the historian-apologist; if pursued further, this thesis becomes so dangerous that it automatically subverts the supernatural in Christianity and the divine in revelation" (PE, p. 192).

[38] "To reach Christ, if He is truly the Word Incarnate, to justify dogma, if it expresses the absolute, we cannot simply trace the course of historical determinism by moving back in time or limit ourselves today to squeezing the meaning out of primitive texts..." (PE, pp. 213-14).

[39] "We waited for Parousia, and the Church came" (PE, p. 182). Cf. A. Loisy, EE, p. 153.

[40] "The more we hope to demonstrate that the coming of the Kingdom was the essence of evangelical teaching, the longer we will deprive Christ of His rights as the Father of the society, in agony, of the pilgrims of this life" (PE, p.184).

[41] What is meant by history, for example, in the statement that in a way Tradition knows "history in a different way and better than the historian", or in the reference to a "reality of divine History that (the Church) strives to resemble" (cf. pp. 200-201, 219)? It seems that history as life, or history as reality is viewed as *transcendent* with respect to the possible approaches that are always a partial illumination of the truth; at the same time, qualifying history as "sacred" connects it to the life of faith, something that can be truly known only in and through the life of faith to the exclusion of the critical method. Blondel holds that history as life "tends to represent substantial reality" (PE, p. 170); whereas history as science, having ensured the respect of dogma, in actual fact "deprives

of this chapter is devoted to the attempt to make them explicit. First of all, "Tradition" has a vital meaning which goes well beyond the normal ken of scientific determination: it is not reduced to the reflected expression, to the intellectual element, which is what can be most easily transferred into *writing*.[42] A new conception of historical factuality also seems necessary, given that we often speak about facts or historical events independently of any historical-scientific understanding of them. It must be admitted, however, that this problem does not receive an adequate answer in this work, especially as the anti-intellectualistic or vitalistic insistence on defining Tradition makes the whole perspective vague (the perspective of a rigorous epistemological determination of a factuality or reality *other* than that of the modern sciences).[43] At times Blondel seems to acknowledge the validity or the legitimacy of critical history, provided it is connected with and, obviously, subordinated to not only theology (as a purely speculative discipline, it too is subordinate) but to Tradition and to the Church — as if theology and Tradition lacked the means of bearing witness to facts; elsewhere he seems to be claiming the opposite.[44] Above all, it seems that

---

it of all outlets, removing even the support of sacred History, so that there will no longer be two different histories, one according to science, the other according to faith" (PE, pp. 199-200).

[42] PE, pp. 203-205. Cf. PE, p. 215: "No, this does not mean rejecting the necessary role of thought, the value of reason... the search for the multiple sources of our spiritual life beneath distinct perceptions, reflective ideas and explicit reasoning".

[43] Blondel reiterates that Tradition links *facts* and *dogmas*; what is not clear, however, is whether these facts are the result of a historical-critical elaboration (perhaps corrected and purified) or whether they are also obtained autonomously. Cf. PE, pp. 205-207: "Something about the Church escapes scientific control; after all it is the Church that controls all the contributions of exegesis and history, always taking them into account and never overlooking them, since she possesses, through the very Tradition of which she is constituted, another means of knowing her author, or participating in His life, of linking facts and dogmas... And so the difficulty hindering us at the outset of this study seems resolved: the principle of synthesis is not in mere facts or ideas, it is in Tradition which encompasses historical data, the efforts of reason and the accumulated experiences of faithful action". Also PE, p. 212: "If the essential truth of Catholicism is the incarnation of dogmatic ideas in historical facts...".

[44] PE, pp. 172-73, 222. Cf. PE, p. 207: "Is it not unusual to claim that after over nineteen centuries there is a method - which is not a totally mystical one - to reach the true Christ...? Will a historian not ridicule this "extrahistorical" means we claim to possess of knowing the consciousness of Jesus and of forming the sacred History of Revelation without the *placet* of criticism?".

the role of historiography is restricted to questions of detail, or particulars, while the overall vision, the perspective in which they are placed, is "extrahistorical" in the sense that it is provided by faith and by the teaching of the Church: the whole, the essential, is Christ who, by emerging more and more distinctly from the mass of data and particulars, allows them to be reorganized and assessed.[45] The theme of the whole and of the part intersects with the anti-intellectualist theme of "the implicit experienced" and of "the explicit realized" in the sense that it is the profound recesses of life and of history that work synthetically *vis à vis* the superficial and purely conceptual multiplicity of doctrines and methods.[46]

Only towards the end of his work does Blondel hint at the decisive theme. The Church is a community that ensures its own truths, that supports its own theses and proves them on the basis of its own testimony. She "is herself proof, *index sui est*, for she embodies in her age-old experience and in constant profession the verification of what she believes and of what she teaches". Regardless of how reality is understood, it is always the product of intersubjective verification, of a *converging*, of the experience of a multiplicity of subjects — this is true for the community of science, but also for the community of faith, which has no need therefore of an external criterion of reference. It "contains an intrinsic force of justification irrespective of historical evidence or of moral appearances; it is important that this internal criterion not be reduced merely to an extrinsic and accessory argument". Ultimately what remains dissonant in modern science as well as in historiography with respect to the experience of faith is that faith is a vital experience which engages the person as a whole, a *collective* experience, whereas science emphasizes an intellectual and *individual* attitude directed exclusively to the *written* text: "... in going from facts to dogmas, the most accurate textual analysis and intellectual effort of the individual are not enough. What is needed is the mediation of collective

---

[45] Cf. PE, p. 220. The main flaw in this reasoning is that history, *per se* a senseless mass of data, is unified and endowed with meaning thanks to a unifying criterion *outside* history; in this respect it barely touches on the true hermeneutical theme.

[46] "In a sense that has been clarified and without denying the legitimate role of discursive thought, it can be said that the passage is from faith to dogmas rather than from dogmas to faith" (PE, p. 218). "Isolating the science of facts or of Christian dogmas from the science of Christian life" is like tearing out "the bride's heart" (PE, p. 222).

life and the slow, progressive work of Christian tradition".[47] Thus, from this point of view, history as science and history as reality appear to be the object-correlates of two different communities. Of course, there is also a rebuke addressed to the Protestant communities for having conceded too much to the modern scientific method by intellectualizing the understanding of faith, or by isolating the individual scholar in a presumed autonomy: in short, by neglecting that ecclesial communion is founded upon expectations and implicit recognitions. "Through erudition or dialectics we will never be able to justify the union of facts and beliefs, as if each reason conducted its dogmatic work alone. To succeed in this justification, it is necessary to take into account the effort of the whole individual being but also the consensus of all the beings who lead the same life and share in the same love".[48]

---

[47] PE, p. 206. "One must no longer seek an individual or merely intellectual criterion to connect facts and beliefs... Dogmas can in no way be justified solely by historical science, nor by dialectics ingeniously applied to texts, nor by the efforts of the individual" (PE, pp. 216-218).

[48] PE, p. 227. This development in Blondel's thought may have been influenced by the "metaphysics of relation", or of love, developed by the Oratorian L. Laberthonnière in those years. Laberthonnière enthusiastically hailed the publication of *Historie et Dogme* at the end of his work on "Christian realism" (cf. L. Laberthonnière, *Le réalisme chrétien, précédé de Essais de philosophie religieuse* [Paris: Ed. du Seuil, 1966] p. 348, note 1).

Bergsonism and Modernism
A. Loisy and the Critique of Christianity

1. It is a known fact that in various periods of European history there have been tensions between mysticism and theology: for example in the fourteenth century with the growth of a "spiritual" literature, which was in part autonomous, or in the sixteenth and seventeenth centuries, with official positions that were all in all negative with regard to mystical experience (Melchior Cano, Bossuet) and the disputes around the notion of "pure love" (between Bossuet and Fénelon, and before that, during the reign of Louis XIII, between Sirmond and Camus, a pupil of St. Francis of Sales).[1] Since the works of H. Bremond it has become almost a commonplace to say that towards the end of the seventeenth century the controversy died down, and whether because of the condemnation of quietism (Fénelon and M.me de Guyon) or for other reasons, silence descended on the problem of mystical experience. And we have to wait for end of the nineteenth century, or the first decades of the twentieth, to find a real "mystical movement" which involves, albeit amidst doubts and renewed controversy, also the status and significance of theology.

The "mystical movement" that developed in France towards the end of the nineteenth century can be linked to a need for interior reflection, as a reaction against the primacy of works of charity and devotion and their humanistic motivations. It is not, however, a matter of seeking refuge in a private or intimate world, or of losing the world (one might think of Thérèse of Lisieux or of Charles de Foucauld), but of an attempt to re-establish, to rediscover Christian essentiality, in a society in which solidarism, or

---

[1]   Cf. H. Bremond, *La querelle du pur amour au temps de Louis XIII. Antoine Sirmond et Jean-Pierre Camus* (Paris, 1932) (Cahiers de la Nouv. Journée, 22).

progressivism, of a positivist kind and the prevailing of an ethical dimension risked being confused with Christianity. Theological reflection on the problem points in two main directions: the first, supported by the Dominican publication *La Vie spirituelle* (that first appeared in Paris in 1919), put forward the arguments of deduction or of speculation, in that the principles of Revelation have their conclusion — in some sense *a priori* — in religious experience; the other, expressed in the *Revue d'Ascétique et de Mystique*, Toulouse, 1920, asked that the problem be considered in its historical and experiential dimension, and that the life of faith be seen as something to which psychological inquiry, and in general the method of positive science, should be applied.

In this alternative the influence of secular culture on the development of the problem can already be noticed. By the twenties and thirties philosophical speculation already makes regular use of the contributions of the scientific disciplines, and as regards religion and mysticism there is a flourishing output of writings around the turn of the century, some of which are later mentioned in the work that without a doubt represents one of the high points of the discussion, *The Two Sources of Morality and Religion* by H. Bergson.[2] In his work, as in that of others, there is the typical tendency to approach the discussion about Christianity from an empirical, experiential point of view and to make of it a discussion about mysticism: this tendency, which was generally contested by the Catholic Church (also because it is close to the arguments of the modernists, in its vitalistic and pragmatistic implications), had an apologetic importance, in that it conformed religion to the dominant scientific mentality or to the positivist ideology. The discussions in the twenties took this connection into consideration, within the framework of the more general problem already encountered during the modernist crisis of the beginning of the twentieth century about the use and the relevance of the human sciences (psychology and history) for the religious sciences.[3] The philosophers and historians

---

[2]   Bergson cites Durkheim, Lévy-Bruhl, Mauss, and, in the context of studies on mysticism, Delacroix (*Etudes d'histoire et de psychologie du mysticisme* [Paris, 1908]) and De Montmorand (*Psychologie des mystiques catholiques orthodoxes* [Paris, 1920]).

[3]   Cf. L. de Grandmaison, "Les hautes études religieuses", in *La vie catholique dans la France contemporaine* (Paris, 1918) pp. 243-304. The main discussions of the twenties are to be found in the *Bulletin de la Société française de la philosophie*, May-June (1925) and January (1926) - contributions by Delacroix, Blondel, Laberthonnière, Baruzi, Le Roy - and in the collective work *Q'est-ce que la mystique?* (Paris, 1925) (Cahiers de la Nouv. Journée, 3) - studies by Blondel, Delbos, Wehrlé, Paliard.

who had lived and suffered the modernist question, who had experienced the condemnations or the mistrust of the Catholic hierarchy, were particularly favourable to a new and more open kind of religious sentiment, free of the bonds of traditional dogma. For them, mysticism is the sign of an encounter, which is anyway positive (and this is the reason for the dissension with the Catholic Church), with modern humanity; that is, with religious experience, also other than Christian (a problem that had been dealt with in Troeltsch's major work)[4] and with the new sciences of man.

But the discussion about mysticism also meant a re-examination or a reformulation of the overall theoretical framework; thus, alongside the scientific works (e.g. ethnological or historical) we find philosophical writings, attempts at formulating a global view like those of Loisy or of Bergson. In fact, the question of mysticism comprises a hermeneutical question (what forms religious experience takes, and to what extent and in what sense doctrinal developments constitute a barrier or are an element of identification of this experience), an anthropological question (the primacy of contemplation or of action), and a question that I am going to call political (the service of God to the exclusion of the world, the service of man to the exclusion of God). If a religion of the future or of humanity is developed, mysticism implies a philosophy of history and therefore leads to a decision about this form of philosophy; moreover, it can also lead to not wholly welcome considerations about the need for easy, sentimental and consolatory ideologies that seems to manifest itself above all in the economically most advanced countries. In this sense, a certain optimistic or evolutionistic superficiality, which can be linked to expectations arising in the areas of technology and of science, is certainly recognizable in the philosophical work of Loisy, and, in a different way, also in the later writings of Bergson ("the essential function of the universe, which is a machine destined to create deities", are his concluding words).

2. In his conception of the historiographical method, or rather of the scientific method, Loisy was bound to the kantian tradition, though it is certain that he never had any direct contacts with either Kant or Hegel;[5] but when, in later years, he was no longer in the Catholic Church and he was elaborating his own moral and religious position, should we still speak

---

[4] I refer to *Die Absolutheit des Christentums und die Religionsgeschichte* (see chapter I, note 17).
[5] Cf. E. Poulat, CM, pp. 181-216 (see chapter I, note 18).

of Kantism? I think we should, even if it is a tricky question and must be examined from various points of view. It is, above all, the Kantism that Loisy absorbed during his study of liberal Protestantism: for example, the idea that the truth, in a metaphysical sense, about God or the world is not accessible to man, or rather that such truth is pointless or harmful; the idea that moral action, the encounter with one's fellow-men, is where truth in a Christian sense is authentically to be found ("the love of one's neighbour is the only practical proof on earth of that love of God which finds its life in humility", writes Harnack in his famous work of 1900); the idea of a progressive humanisation or moralisation of the great religions, in particular of Christianity. Loisy could easily have found all this in Sabatier, Harnack and Troeltsch.[6] Moreover, Loisy's anti-metaphysical and anti-scholastic tendency puts him very close to the Protestants in the sense that, even if he continues to reject their "individualism",[7] fundamentally he shares their view about the possibility, or necessity, of reconciling Christianity and the modern world through a relativisation of doctrinal formulas and a re-evaluation of a lived faith, or of religious experience; and in this we can see the influence, direct or indirect, of Schleiermacher of the *Speeches*, so frequently quoted by Sabatier and whose presence is clearly felt also in Harnack's position.[8]

But, unless we want to renew the myth of the traitor, of the renegade acting on behalf of Germany (where political betrayal becomes, as it were, only the outer covering, the perceptible body, of religious betrayal), then we must also consider the French roots of this thinker who contested the Protestant sense of interiority and constantly stressed the collective, public and social nature of religion. Loisy's relationship of concord-discord with the Sociological School and with Durkheim has not yet been studied but it is certain that Loisy conceived of the social nature of religion in a different way from Durkheim, for he refused to absorb religion into society.[9] While positivist scientism thought it possible to trace the religious back to the social and the social back to the rational (through the development of the

---

6   Cf. A. Harnack, WC, p. 75 (see chapter II, note 1).
7   Cf. A. Firmin (A. Loisy), "La théorie individualiste de la religion (for Sabatier)", *Revue du clergé français* (1 January 1899) pp. 202-214; A. Loisy, EE-GC (for Harnack) (see chapter IV, notes 1 e 13).
8   Cf. A. Sabatier, *Esquisse d'une philosophie de la religion d'après la psychologie et l'histoire* cit., pp. 14-15, 19-20, 25, 30, 196-97.
9   Cf. A. Firmin (A. Loisy), "La définition de la religion", *Revue du clergé français* (15 February 1899) pp. 526-557.

new anthropological sciences), Loisy held the inverse position: the rational is founded in the social (and thus is essentially *historical*: critical of metaphysics), and both of these are founded in the intuitive (and beyond the rational) life of the religious experience of humanity. Léonce de Grandmaison wrote: "We would have a more precise idea of the modernist spirit if we said that its supporters, despairing of dogmatic truth in a traditional sense... made every effort to maintain the *psychology* and the *sociology* of Catholicism while sacrificing what we should not be afraid to call its *metaphysics*".[10]

As a historian Loisy was a disciple of Renan, and he had studied his conception of Messianic hope.[11] Moreover, after his excommunication he had clarified better his philosophical position, which was that of a "religion of humanity" closely linked to the themes of the philosophy of history of the late nineteenth century.[12] Did Loisy know Comte? In June 1904 he wrote in a note: "Comte was not altogether wrong with his cult of humanity. For us humanity is the supreme revelation of God".[13] But he had not read his work; what he knew about him was second-hand. Writing to Boyer de Sainte Suzanne on 14 July 1922 he said, "I do not see how there could be a close connection between my conception of the religion of humanity and that of Comte, given that our notions of religion, of the law and of humanity are so different from each other".[14] But he also said he preferred "Comte with his religion of humanity" to "Renan with his religion of science... *scientism* is a heresy to be condemned" (to Boyer, 3 March 1919). In actual fact, Loisy mistrusted the metaphysical and authoritarian (old-Catholic) nature of the founder of Positivism; his criticisms of Comte's systematic, "metaphysical and scholastic" approach, which tended to become fixed in an orthodoxy hostile to research, were the same criticisms he had always made of Thomist philosophy (letters to Boyer dated 26 October 1919 and 14 July 1922).[15] On the other hand, what Loisy objected to in Renan was a

---

[10] L. de Grandmaison, *Christus. Manuel d'histoire des religions* (Paris, 1912) p. 983.

[11] "L'espérance messianique d'après E. Renan", *Revue d'histoire et de littérature religieuses* 5 (1898) pp. 385-406 (then in *Etudes bibliques*, III ed., Paris 1903, pp. 260-89).

[12] According to H. Gouhier, it is the part of his work "that carries the most visible signs of the waning XIXth century". Preface to: R. de Boyer de Sainte Suzanne, *A. Loisy entre la foi et l'incroyance* (Paris, 1968) p. 10 (henceforth referred to as BS).

[13] Cf. *Mémoires pour servir à l'histoire religieuse de notre temps*, II (Paris, 1930) p. 402.

[14] BS, p. 22

[15] BS, pp. 194, 228-29.

certain scepticism, an aristocratic detachment: "His attitude towards the
wretchedness of men was rather like that of Anatole France: sneering and
indulgent contempt... all he did was to complain about the decline of
morality in contemporary society. 'We are living on the shadow of a shadow;
what will people after us live on?' And he never actually said what people
would be able to live on" (to Boyer, 3 October 1920).[16] It can be surmised
that, even if in 1917 (when his important work *La religion* came out) Loisy
had still not read a single line of Comte (letter to Miss Petre of 23 October
1917), he knew Renan's positions extremely well, including the passage in
L'avenir de la science in which Renan confessed: "It is my intimate conviction
that the religion of the future will be pure humanism, which means the
cult of all that is human, the whole of life sanctified and raised to a moral
value". He may have read Bergson's account of French philosophy (1915),
where it is stated that "Renan, intellectually speaking, is not akin to Comte"
but "in his own way, and in a totally different way, he too believed in this
religion of humanity that the founder of Positivism had dreamt of".[17]

There is another element contributing to Loisy's formation that
seems to me somewhat mysterious and that has not been studied
specifically. The best historiography has linked his insistence on morality
to his Protestant and neo-kantian formation, but it is clear that this insistence
(which is also a search for simplicity or for truth, and is critical of the vain
constructions of theologians) has roots much further back in modern culture. What I am referring to is the Enlightenment, understood above all as
the turning-point of an age and a lesson in method, in both philosophy
and the sciences (which is how certain Protestants, e.g. Troeltsch, and some
French Catholics, e.g. Blondel, understood it).[18] When Loisy writes (in 1924)
that "it is much less important to speculate on the nature of the spirit, on
the possibility of its transcendence, and on the features of its immanence

---

[16] BS, p. 204
[17] Cf. M.D. Petre, *A. Loisy. Its Religious Significance* (Cambridge, 1944) pp. 118-
      119; E. Renan, *Oeuvres complètes*, III, Paris, p. 809; H. Bergson, "La philosophie
      française", *La Revue de Paris* (15 mai 1915) pp. 236 ff.; CM, pp. 233-35.
[18] Cf. E. Troeltsch, *Aufklärung*, in *Realenzyklopädie für protestantische Theologie und
      Kirche*, II, 1897, pp. 225-41; later in *Gesammelte Schriften*, IV (Tübingen, 1925;
      Aalen: Scientia, 1981). Blondel gives his opinion about the irreversibility of the
      Enlightenment transformation of modern reason (and the consequent vanity
      of the Aristotelian-Thomist "rebirths") in particular in his *Letter on Apologetics*
      of 1896 ("Lettre sur les exigences de la pensée contemporaine en matière
      d'apologétique et sur la méthode de la philosophie dans l'étude du problème
      religieux", in PE, pp. 5-95).

than to contribute to the work of the spirit and to its coming, and to participate in it", we are moving irremediably in the direction of Rousseau's *Profession de foi du vicaire savoyard*, where we read: "I try to know only what is important for my conduct. As for dogmas, they affect neither our actions nor our morality and many people torment themselves over them, but they leave me completely indifferent".[19]

      3. Bergson got to know Loisy personally in 1908, when Loisy was standing for election at the Collège de France. Before 1905 (before he had read Paul Desjardins' book about Loisy, *Catholicisme et critique*), Bergson knew very little about him, but had evidently heard the rumours circulating at the time about a sort of Protestant masquerading as a Catholic (his letter to Desjardins: "I imagined (his work) to be similar to that of Sabatier"); but in 1909, he was to be one of Loisy's grand electors at the Collège de France, and he even accepted to review the draft of his inaugural lecture.[20] But it was not until later, after 1917 (when the first edition of *La religion* was published), that Bergson began to write a series of philosophically significant letters to Loisy (which Loisy reacted to either by writing to Boyer de Sainte Suzanne, or, above all, by publishing other works). Basing ourselves on these letters we will now try to focus on the philosophical personality of Loisy through the picture that Bergson had of him. After Loisy had sent him the book, Bergson wrote (2 July 1917): "If I had to point to the idea that, after a first reading, seems to me central, I would say it is that most profound conception of faith you have. It illuminates what you say about the connection between religion and religions as well as that between religion and morality".[21] The conception of faith that Bergson was referring to is what Bremond, in a work on Loisy published under a

---

[19] Cf. A. Loisy, *Religion et humanité* (Paris, 1926) pp. 197-98; J.-J. Rousseau, *Oeuvres complètes*, IV (Paris, 1969) pp. 625-27. I have dealt with Rousseau's religious position in the chapter on *Emile* in my book, *Alienazione e storia. Saggio su Rousseau* (Bologna: Il Mulino, 1976) pp. 99-132.

[20] Cf. CM, p. 256 and E. Poulat, *Modernistica. Horizons, Physionomies, Débats* (Paris, 1982) p. 133. *Catholicisme et critique* (with the subtitle: *Réflexions d'un profane sur l'affaire Loisy*) was published in Paris, in 1905, by the *Cahiers de la Quinzaine*. The inaugural lecture of the course of history of religions at the Collège de France was given on 3 May 1909, but the printed version (Paris, 1909) bears the date 24 April. The letter from Bergson approving the text was written on 7 February.

[21] CM, p. 257.

pseudonym[22], called "mysticism", which he set in opposition to "dogmatic" faith. It is a faith that does not stop at the doctrinal formula set down by a positive religion, but it cuts right across the formula and aims at the very truth or reality of the divine or of the spirit, at the essence of religion. In short, both authors acknowledge a supra-rational faculty that puts man in relation with the ultimate or most profound realities: Loisy calls this faculty "religious sentiment", "faith" or "intuition" ("what Bergson called intuition I call faith" he wrote to Boyer on 27 February, 1918, probably after reading *L'Evolution créatrice*).[23] And both of them compare this faculty or function with an inferior or secondary activity, that of conceptual or intellectual determination, to which the sphere of dogmatic definitions also belongs. But Loisy claims to be more sensitive to the experience of faith (which is mobile and in the course of becoming) than to the grand constructions or visions of the world; he feels he is more an historian than a theologian, more a mystic than a philosopher. And it is this, in the end, that separates him from Bergson: mysticism is, both for him and for Bergson, "the principle and the basis of all spiritual life", but then their ways part. Mysticism (in the sense of faith or intuition that surpasses every conceptual determination) is "essentially something other than metaphysics" and it makes no sense to make it part of a universal philosophy of life and of the spirit.[24] Loisy's mistrust of metaphysics, and of theology, derives from the fact that in his opinion they do not respect the mobility of reality: they immobilise thought in definitive formulas and make doctrine prevail over faith.[25]

Was he then a traitor if he stayed in the Catholic Church for so long? The controversy that raged over this question has never really abated: the early historians of modernism upheld the thesis of his evident duplicity and falsity,[26] while it was Bremond who (anonymously) argued most

---

[22]   Cf. S. Leblanc (H. Bremond), *Un clerc qui n'a pas trahi. A. Loisy d'après ses Mémoires (1931)*, ed. E. Poulat (Rome, 1972) (henceforth referred to as SL).

[23]   Cf. *Mémoires*, cit., II, p. 588 (letter to Merry del Val of 29 September 1907) and BS, p. 122.

[24]   Cf. A. Loisy, *G. Tyrrell et H. Bremond* (Paris, 1936) pp. 189-190 (henceforth TB). Speaking of Comte (but maybe also with Bergson in mind) he had stated, for example, that while Comte denied the existence of any spiritual life to come, he affirmed its existence but "without defining it" (M.D. Petre, *A. Loisy*, cit., pp. 118-19).

[25]   A. Loisy, *La morale humaine* (Paris, 1928) p. 127.

[26]   A. Houtin, *Histoire du modernisme catholique* (Paris, 1913); J. Rivière, *Le modernisme dans l'Eglise* (Paris, 1929).

strongly in his favour, distinguishing between dogmatic faith and mystical faith. In my view, however, there were no fundamental modifications in Loisy's intellectual evolution. In 1883 (aged 26) he was thinking about "a general reform of Catholic teaching, based on the notion of the relativity of beliefs, which would have saved the substance of these obsolete beliefs". Already at that time he associated the problem of religious faith with the historical or hermeneutical problem, in the sense that he recognised the relativity of every truth accessible to man and placed the absolute or God in an infinitely superior, unapproachable and incomprehensible zone. The irreparable conflict with Catholic orthodoxy was, he remembers, already evident in the winter of 1885-86, though he did not yet reject (according to the dualistic kernel-husk, essence-manifestation pattern) "the substance of truth which must be admitted to be the ultimate foundation of Christian and Catholic tradition".[27] It is this that Bremond calls "mystical faith" and that at a certain point, according to his loyal friend, takes the place of the dogmatic faith of his ecclesiastical formation. But when did this happen? As I said, this transformation is difficult to identify: Loisy always saw his relationship with the Catholic Church in a context in which the most frequently used terms are society, humanity and progress. He wanted a reform that would link the Church to contemporary culture and transform it into a sort of pedagogical institution, at the service of the spiritual and moral development of a new humanity.[28] It is true that a further transformation came about with his separation, partly imposed on him and partly willed by him, from the Catholic Church: after 1908 it no longer seemed to him to be the main agent of renewal. In his presentation of a short work by Sylvain Leblanc, Loisy presents himself as a person who "having broken away from theological dogmatism in 1886, had wanted to loyally serve the Church as an educative institution of humanity of a religious and moral order, until he felt it was no longer possible to do so without a loss of sincerity". Poulat comments: "between 1886 and 1908 and beyond, at what particular moment did the break with 'theological dogmatism' become the denial of 'Christian faith?'"; but this "Christian faith" consisted above all in a "mystical faith" and a belief, which could

---

[27]   Cf. A. Loisy, *De la croyance à la foi* (1936), in CM, pp. 19-21 (an autobiographical work first published in English in *Religion in Transition* [New York-London 1937], pp. 126-72).

[28]   See the letters of Boyer of 15 November 1917 (BS, p. 185) and 13 July 1919 (BS, p. 166). "He is truly a Noah, and the Church will be overjoyed to have his Ark", wrote Bremond to Blondel on 23 May 1904, CCM, p. 221 (see chapter IV, note 3).

have been sociological-positivist and not really theological, in the Church as an agent of progress.[29] According to *L'Osservatore romano* of 29 June 1940, Loisy had already lost his Christian faith in 1904, and therefore there is obscurity and ambiguity in his behaviour (he celebrated Mass until 1906); he wanted to empty the dogmas, eliminate Christ and make the Church a universal mutual aid association.[30]

In fact, the influence of liberal Protestantism on his "mystical faith" led to a certain vitalism, in which it is increasingly difficult to identify the object of the religious sentiment.[31] According to Bremond, in 1904 Loisy "has already lost his faith, if by faith we mean the adherence of the spirit to revealed dogma. But he has not lost his faith if with this expression we mean a profound, supra-rational, in a word mystical, adherence of his whole being to the invisible realities of which he still believes the Catholic Church to be the main and indispensable guardian".[32] This is his position from 1886 until 1908, the time when he loses his "mystical faith" *in the Church* and moves beyond Christianity towards a religion of humanity. But already a priest who had received the book by Bremond-Leblanc had commented somewhat brutally on the vagueness and inconsistency of Loisy's notions of faith, mysticism and the Church: "in the eyes of one who defines faith a kind of trust, the most ardent atheists are religious, given that it is impossible to conceive of a man who loves nothing... The Church, as Loisy conceives of it, would have no other heretic — if this monstrosity were not impossible — but the perfect egoist, he who takes interest only in himself".[33] These consequences were not to be avoided, given the notion (wrote Bremond, echoing Loisy) "of the relative value of all general theories and thus of the more or less symbolic, opportune and provisional nature that not only the theological systems but also the dogmas aquire". "This is where I find myself still convinced of the need for religion, of the divine nature of Christianity", wrote Loisy as late as 1930, but also of the impossibility, for the Catholic Church, of grasping and immobilising the absolute in its formulas.[34]

---

[29] Cf. SL, pp. 68-69.

[30] SL, pp. 85-86.

[31] Harnack writes, recalling Schleiermacher: "It is only the religion which a man himself has experienced that is to be confessed... If there is no broad 'doctrine of religion' to be found in the Gospel, still less is there any direction that a man is to begin by accepting and confessing any ready-made doctrine" (WC, p.151).

[32] SL, p. 148.

[33] Letter of abbé Bernard to the editor Nourry, 20 October 1931 (SL, pp. 75-76).

[34] Cf. SL, p. 128 and A. Loisy, *Mémoires*, cit., I (1930) p. 136. Loisy wrote in his diary (31 May 1905): "No-one is orthodox. Orthodoxy is the fancy of those

On the other hand, on the positive side, one can notice the attention that this conception of faith gave to the problem of testimony (probably with the incentive of vitalistic and pragmatic motivations that were already widespread in French culture).[35] The criticism of dogmatic faith includes the criticism of scholastic objectivism or intellectualism ("the adherence of the spirit to revealed dogmas" is the expression Bremond uses, that is to say, to the precise *form* with which the Church chooses to express them); whereas the choice of mystical faith includes a practical-ascetic indication ("adherence of the whole being") and a reference to the profound supra-rational forces that put us in communication with the divine.[36] But this conception was not Loisy's alone: it was shared by Bremond and was to be found, in various forms, in the whole modernist movement. Dogmatic faith was rejected because it could not be reconciled with science and with modern (post-Enlightenment) culture. Mystical faith was acknowledged because it could be reconciled with science or with its fundamental assumption — the changeability, the evolution of every reality. Even a man like père Laberthonnière, whose loyalty to the Catholic Church was total (also through a kind of martyrdom), had distinguished, in his work on the mysticism of Monsignor Gay, between an abstract, purely objective truth of scholastic theology and a lived, creatively reconstructed or subjective truth of mystical experience. And of course mystics were the true religious men, because life, or rather action, is the decisive element of our religion, as this admirable phrase shows: "to have faith is to believe in love".[37] Unlike Laberthonnière, Loisy had developed these themes in a post-Christian way, as if Christianity was at that point a hindrance or a limitation to the full achievement of human solidarity. It is this faith "which is not dogmatic, but is religious in the strict sense" that represents the final evolution of

---

who have never thought for themselves" (*Mémoires*, III (1931) p. 391).

[35] Cf. J. Bourdeau, *Pragmatisme et modernisme* (Paris, 1909); A. Leclère, *Pragmatisme, modernisme, protestantisme* (Paris, 1909); G. Gentile, "Religione e pragmatismo", in *Il modernismo e i rapporti fra religione e filosofia* (Bari, 1921); R. Berthelot, *Le pragmatisme religieux chez W. James et chez les catholiques modernistes* (Paris, 1922). These trends had been largely absorbed into Loisy's writings, as for example the following passage shows: "but if abstract dogmas are of no import, religious practices are something like sources of beneficial emotions. The Christian ideal lives and takes effect in the ceremonies of worship..."; (*Mémoires*, I [1930] p.365).

[36] SL, p. 148.

[37] L. Laberthonnière, "Un mystique au XIX siècle", *La Quinzaine* 5 (1 August 1899) vol.29, no. 115, pp. 297-310; later in *Essais de philosophie religieuse* (Paris, 1903) pp. 291-309. Later on, Laberthonnière took part, together with Le Roy, in the

"mystical faith" after all denominational loyalties have been abandoned.[38]

Let us now return to the letter of Bergson. "Concerning this last point, the relationship of morality to religion, I too had been working for a number of years on some research and thoughts that were interrupted by the war. Thanks to a kind of preordained harmony, I had reached conclusions which at least in part concord with yours and which, where there is this concordance, are so similar to yours that, in my notes, they are expressed in virtually identical terms. Perhaps the similarity has to do with the fact that both of us make a fundamental distinction between life itself, the essence of which is mobility, and living forms through which life merely passes".[39] Bergson attributed his own metaphysical vision to Loisy, but this was only partially possible: it is true that Loisy always asserted the mutability or becoming of every reality and the supremacy of intuition and faith, or at any rate of suprarational forces, over reason and science; but he also fought against metaphysics, denying that the most profound reality is accessible to man. This is to say that Loisy set up a dualistic system similar to that of Bergson (history-theology, experiential-doctrinal, alive-established, dynamic-static), but one in which what is knowable and accessible is only the experiential-dynamic side, or the *manifestation* of that ultimate reality that philosophy (metaphysics) and theology try in vain to grasp with their formulas. The dynamic or the live aspect that Loisy seeks is superficial, the object of observation of the historian, while what Bergson seeks is profound, beyond the reach of the human sciences and accessible only to metaphysics. It is true that both refer to religious experience, to mysticism which is "the soul of religion and of morality", but for Loisy the

---

debate on mysticism held at the French Philosophical Society based on a review by J. Baruzi, "St. Jean de la Croix et le problème de la valeur noétique de l'expérience mystique" (2 May 1925). Cf. *Bulletin de la Société française de philosophie* 25 (1925) nos. 2-3, pp. 43-75; reproduced in *Esquisse d'une philosophie personnaliste* (Paris, 1942) pp. 645-87.

[38] SL, pp. 161-62, cf. *Mémoires*, cit., III (1931) p. 301: "I begin to perceive the new God, who will be a better ideal of humanity than Christ, yes, better and truer than Christ, whose place must be taken by the mere dedication *usque ad mortem* to the ideal perceived". Loisy had given Bremond an excerpt that was to have been the conclusion of Bremond-Leblanc's work, and which served to confirm his extraneousness to the Catholic Church: "the triumph of modernism can only be in the fall of orthodoxy; and the disappearance of orthodoxy also means that of traditional Christianity, because it is the best of all religions - and not only of Catholicism - that must survive in the religion of humanity" (SL, pp. 66 and 181).

[39] CM, p. 257.

deepening of this experience will always lead to other experiences, to other men, and will tell us nothing of what exists beyond time and the world we know.[40] Bergson goes on: "I would not say, however, that I agree completely with you on the question of the relationship between religion and morality. The divergence of opinion that is already evident here would increase on other points. It is connected with the greater importance that I would attribute to *mystical experience*. I would give morality, and also religion, more of a *metaphysical* foundation than you".[41] Here we are introduced to a new theme that needs serious consideration. Bergson no longer attributes his metaphysical vision to Loisy but he asks him to take a stand on the subject of metaphysics; he asks him if mystical experience, duly examined in depth and seen basically to converge, should not lead us to believe in the existence of the God that mystics encounter.[42] We have seen how Loisy is still attached to a kind of metaphysical agnosticism that is connected with his sense of science and of historical criticism. In Bergson's opinion he was in some way unable to escape from this historical-critical attitude and he had no sensitivity, or intimate feeling, for religion.[43] The fact is that the two men were going in different directions: Bergson was moving closer to Christianity (as was to become clear in his book of 1932, *The Two Sources of Morality and Religion*), while Loisy was moving away from it. For Bergson the concordance of the great Christian mystics pointed to the existence of

---

[40]   See A. Loisy, *La religion* (Paris, 1924) p. 5. Cf. A. Houtin, F. Sartiaux, *A. Loisy. Sa vie, son oeuvre*, ed. E. Poulat (Paris, 1960) pp. 251-52: "the eternal religion that Loisy attempted to discover gradually became... a mysterious, undefinable *entity* that bears humanity, raises it, urges it along the way of Human progress. This metaphysical elaboration is extended, under Bergson's influence, into a kind of *ontology*, which binds morals and religion in a universal dynamism". I do not agree with this interpretation, except in the sense that L. may have absorbed a new sense of the "spirit" as activity and movement from writings of Bergson like *L'énergie spirituelle* (1920) or *L'évolution créatrice*, which he read in 1917 (letter to Boyer of 27 February 1918, BS, pp. 186-89).

[41]   CM, p. 257.

[42]   "The surprising *convergence* of their testimonies can only be explained by the *existence* of what they experienced" (to Chevalier, 8 March 1932. Cf. J. Chevalier, *Entretiens avec Bergson* [Paris, 1959] pp. 152-58). "The experience of the great Catholic mystics gives them the indestructible conviction of their survival... Their agreement on this point, and others just as surprising, would find a satisfactory explanation in the reality of the object in which they believe" (to Magnin, 7 January 1933, cf. CM, p. 320). Similar declarations are to be found in H. Bergson, *The Two Sources of Morality and Religion*, trans. by R. Ashley Audra & Cloudesley Brereton (London, 1935) (henceforth referred to as MR).

[43]   Cf. J. Guitton, *La vocation de Bergson* (Paris, 1960) pp. 180-81.

the object they speak of, a supreme and invisible reality; for Loisy religion was above all a historical phenomenon, the moral and social life of humanity.

These differences were pointed out by Loisy in a series of letters to his young friend Boyer de Sainte Suzanne: the inadequacy of our information, the limits of intelligence, everything concurs to make us cautious about the metaphysical question, which, in typical Rousseau fashion, he indicates as "secondary" compared with the practical or ethical question. Loisy wrote, "The famous philosopher whom you mention in your letter wrote to me about my last book, saying that he would give more importance than I do to metaphysics as the foundation of morality. It seems to me that learned metaphysics is more the crowning than the basis of the formation of men. My aim was to construct a discipline of life that was in no way based on an always questionable cosmological theory". Certainly, we would like to know if there exists an eternal life, a God who loves us and guides humanity, but all these questions go beyond human possibilities and, at most, will lead to hypotheses but never to definite certainties (to Boyer, 6 October 1917).[44] In the same period (23 October) he wrote the letter already mentioned to Miss Petre in which, speaking of Comte, he admits the possibility of affirming the existence of a "spiritual life to come", but "without defining it", and writing to von Hügel (15 January 1918) he confirms that he does not mean to deny "the existence of any superhuman reality" but only our human capacity for understanding these things: "It is not only the fault of men if they no longer see clearly. The beginning of wisdom for them would perhaps be not to presume to know what they do not know".[45]

---

[44] BS, pp. 181-82. The same themes are repeated, with almost the same words, in the second letter about Bergson (to Boyer, 27 February 1918, BS, pp. 186-89), and in two other later letters in which Bergson's name is not mentioned (to Boyer, 29 May and 13 June 1918, BS, pp. 192-93). Loisy believes that the merely conjectural nature of metaphysical hypotheses appeared only recently to the consciousness of humanity, and that *progress* consists also in this limitation of the claims of intelligence (letter to Boyer, 20 February 1919, BS, p. 116).

[45] Cf. M.D. Petre, pp. 118-119; A. Loisy, *Mémoires*, cit., III (1931) p. 352. This position stays basically unchanged in the evolution of Loisy, but even in his writings occasional attempts at a definition of the absolute can be found: "the mysterious, sacred power, which has been personified in our forefathers, the spirits, the gods, God - ... the power of the spirit, the soul of righteousness and goodness, the soul of humanity that acts in human societies" (*Religion et humanité* [Paris, 1926] p. 167). Or: "Mysticism... is not the sensible vision or conceptual revelation of a heavenly other world; it is the intuitive sentiment of a present other world,

Going back to Bergson, Loisy comments on the controversy over his evolutionistic Pantheism and Bergson's letter of defence to père de Tonquédec.[46] In *L'évolution créatrice* Loisy sees more "a form of Pantheism" than a picture of the Christian God, but declares himself to be essentially in agreement with Bergson's theory of knowledge: "he is completely right in his critique of pure reason and of science. But I call *faith* what he calls *intuition*, because in my opinion it is more a profound presentiment of realities than a definite perception of them". But for Loisy there is an incomprehensible gulf between this and the construction of a metaphysical system — even if it is connected to that gnoseology: "I no longer understand it". The end result is, as we already know, a religion of humanity or of the future: Loisy "does not deny God", because these words have meant too many things, but he thinks that "God, in a philosophical sense, as first principle of the universe, is inconceivable". On the other hand, God in a historical sense, in a Christian sense, "disappeared with the conception of the world and of history of which He was the supreme expression". The religion of the future will retain much of the Christian past, but not this metaphysical personification of universal being. "We are not obliged, once again, to know the last word on things, because we are incapable of it; but we can give assistance, however little, to humanity. God is love, say the Scriptures, and so love, dedication to humanity, is God Himself, or religion".[47]

Bergson wrote to Loisy on other occasions, especially after receiving his books; on 18 March 1925 he commented on *La morale humaine* and on 27 April 1926 on *Religion et humanité*. If we examine these letters carefully what we find is an abbreviated repetition of the letter of 2 July 1917: cordiality, amazement at the convergence of their positions and elegant dissent on basic questions. "I would tend, in fact, not to take into consideration only the social point of view. I would leave more room for

---

of an infinite in which the consciousness of the self is momentarily absorbed... the rejection of the animality in man... to the advantage of humanity, of the spirit disinterested and devoted" (*La religion* [Paris, 1924] p. 37).

[46] Part of Bergson's letter was published by père de Tonquédec in *Etudes* (20 February 1912), pp. 506 ff., and later in his book *Sur la philosophie bergsonienne* (Paris, 1936). For this discussion, see C. Tresmontant, *La crise moderniste* (Paris, 1979) Ch. IV ("Bergson et les chrétiens", pp. 142-83) that refers all the aspects of the opposition Bergsonism-Christianity back to Bergson's neo-Platonism, in particular to his theory of individuation through matter criticised by p. Laberthonnière).

[47] Letter to Boyer of 27 February 1918 (BS, pp. 186-89).

metaphysical considerations, which seem to me to be equally evident from the facts". Or: "the divergent opinions are, I think, above all about the the role metaphysics should have in creating this (human) ideal".[48] Bergson planned to construct an experimental metaphysics, and so he could reproach Loisy for believing too little in metaphysics and for not giving enough credence to experience; but all this was to emerge clearly only with the publication of his book in 1932, even though it is apparent — and this is one of the peculiar features of this debate — that the enormously long gestation of the book secretly dominates the discussion.[49] The theoretical substance of their relationship is to be found not in their letters but in their books: Bergson's *The Two Sources* and the last two works of Loisy, *Y a-t-il deux sources de la religion et de la morale?*, of 1933, and *G. Tyrrell et H. Bremond* of 1936. Bergson replied to these critical analyses of his metaphysics by letter (12 November 1933 and 16 December 1936), appealing mainly to the difference of outlook and formation that separated the philosopher from the historian (yet had he himself not encouraged the *philosophical* work of Loisy?),[50] and insisting on "the radical difference of nature (and not only of degree, as you seem to believe) between the great mystic and common men".[51] But this statement presupposes a knowledge, even if superficial, of the last great work of Bergson.

4. In *The Two Sources of Morality and Religion* Bergson argues that there exist two types of religion. One, which is *static*, is a means of social preservation, it structures the relations of individuals with each other (and of each individual with himself), and if it preaches love or solidarity its aim is to make the group more united against the enemy; it thus follows the direction of nature, or rather, it translates what would be natural instinct

---

[48] CM, pp. 258-59.

[49] Bergson's book had not been pre-announced: "One fine day, without publicity, without press releases, without anyone being told, not even the author's closest friends, the work people had been awaiting for 25 years appeared in the bookshops" (J. Maritain, *De Bergson à Thomas d'Aquin* [Paris, 1947] p.64).

[50] "You speak of abandoning, at least for the moment, the publication of your philosophical and moral works... I trust that you will persevere in the direction that you have been following for several years, and that just when society is trying to find its orientation, you do not consider your role exhausted" (23 June 1919, cf. CM, pp. 257-58). "How can you face such a formidable task of erudition, and such a constant and penetrating effort of philosophical reflection?" (12 December 1922, cf. CM, p. 258).

[51] CM, p. 259.

onto a social plane (through moral obligation). The other, which is *dynamic*, is in a certain sense contrary to nature as it teaches universal love that extends to the whole of humanity and therefore involves a radical change of outlook and attitude. There is thus a lower, or earlier, level in which religion deceiptfully pursues certain social aims, the two main ones being to turn the individual away from egoism and to turn his thoughts away from death, in order to counteract the destructive power of intelligence (that is, of a critical, scientific way of thinking).[52] But after this phase, in which *obligation* dominates (Bergson excludes any rationalistic interpretation of obligation because reasonings can always be countered by other reasonings),[53] there should come a phase in which justice (which was once just one obligation among many others) emerges as the fundamental value of a "mystical society", which would comprise the whole of humanity. Between these two phases there is, as it were, an incomprehensible *leap*, and this is clear from the fact that religion, originally, does no more than transform the egoism of the individual into the egoism of a group, without eliminating it: loyalty to one's family, to one's country or to one's city. Disinterested love, love that is devotion (which for Loisy is somehow naturally present in humanity given that it coincides with his concept of moral and social life) is for Bergson unheard-of, it is something that humanity is incapable of by itself.[54]

However, in an almost casual example Bergson gives, we can perceive a difficult question that this book poses. Bergson states that the universality of what is human can be reached also "through Reason, in whose communion we are all partakers", through the practice of philosophy.[55] What, then, are we to think? Is love, universal respect, a transformation brought about in us by God, a gift, or is it something that is already present in our vital structure and that maybe simply needs to be made manifest? It would appear that Bergson's evolutionism considers

---

[52] MR, pp. 99-115, 175. Cf. p. 117, where religious representations are seen as "defensive reactions of nature against the representation, by the intelligence, of a depressing margin of the unexpected between the initiative taken and the effect desired".

[53] MR, p. 69.

[54] MR, pp. 21-22: "between the nation, however big, and humanity, there lies the whole distance, from the finite to the indefinite, from the closed to the open... the difference between the two objects is one of kind, not simply one of degree... it is only through God, in God, that religion bids man love mankind" (cf. pp.229, 231).

[55] MR, p. 22.

religion, even dynamic religion, as a movement of man, which originates in man (even if he describes it as a superior or exceptional movement). But humanity is driven by a force that remains the same, *life* which is ordered in a "nature", and which tends to break out of that order as it moves forward: "If society is self-sufficient, it is the supreme authority. But if it is only one of the aspects of life, we can easily conceive that life, which has had to set down the human species at a certain point of its evolution, imparts a new impetus to exceptional individuals who have immersed themselves anew in it, so that they can help society further along its way".[56] Thus, when we say that dynamic religion moves in the opposite direction to nature (that the "purely dynamic" is not "intended by nature" as the purely static is, but is "a contribution of man's genius")[57] we must make our meaning clear: nature is not life, nature is the general shape that life has acquired in one phase of its evolution. "True, if we went down to the roots of nature itself, we might find that it is the same force, manifesting itself directly, as it rotates on its own axis, in the human species once constituted, and subsequently acting indirectly... in order to drive humanity forward". In the case of the superior morality, it is not that any kind of obligation is eliminated, but it is no longer founded on a certain organisation of life, but in life itself at its well-spring, or in life as "vital impetus": now "the primitive impetus here comes into play directly, and no longer through the means of the mechanisms it had set up, and at which it had provisionally halted".[58] It therefore seems a paradox to say that the second part of morality "had no place in nature's plan", given that it too is the result of the same "primitive impetus" or "élan", which shows itself here for the first time directly. But we have already seen what Bergson means by "nature" and in fact he clarifies this situation very precisely: "Hence in passing from social solidarity to the brotherhood of man we break with one particular nature but not with all nature. It might be said... that it is to get back to *natura naturans* that we break away from *natura naturata*".[59] It follows that when

---

[56] MR, p. 82. Cf. p. 182: "we can only understand the evolution of life... if we view it as seeking for something beyond its reach".

[57] MR, pp. 49-50. Cf. p. 190: static religion is "foreshadowed in nature", dynamic religion is "a leap beyond nature".

[58] MR, pp. 38, 42-43.

[59] MR, pp. 44-45. Cf. pp. 79, 82: "The duality itself merges into a unity, for 'social pressure' and 'impetus of love' are but two complementary manifestations of life... Let us then give to the word biology the very wide meaning it should have, and will perhaps have one day, and let us say in conclusion that all morality, be it pressure or aspiration, is in essence biological".

we compare the universality of religion or of love with the universality of philosophy or of reason, the realities we face are not of the same value, neither do they act on the same plane. The *orders* of rationality, law and morality only exist in as much as they are the fixation or partial fall of a principle that is essentially creative, in movement. "Let us not then merely assert that reason... compels our respect and commands our obedience by virtue of its paramount value. We must add that there are, behind reason, the men who have made mankind divine, and who have thus stamped a divine character on reason, which is the essential attribute of man".[60]

It remains to be seen what this vital principle really is, whether it is God or a manifestation, an expression of the divine. This kind of problem could be one of those insoluble, strictly metaphysical, questions, the solution of which is, in Loisy's opinion, of no interest for moral life. For Bergson, mysticism is the means by which "one or more privileged souls" arrive at the ultimate significance of reality and the principle of life. It is, obviously, an effort that surpasses nature, a kind of miracle performed by the "man of genius", or at least by the "highest part of mankind", which has "broken the circle, drawing society in its wake".[61] True mysticism is rare or exceptional: it expresses the profound intention of life to go beyond mankind as an already formed species, and it can exist only through special individuals capable of drawing close to the very sources of being and experiencing its essential meaning. "True mystics simply open their souls to the oncoming wave. Sure of themselves because they feel within them something better than themselves, they prove to be great men of action, to the surprise of those for whom mysticism is nothing but visions and raptures and ecstasies. That which they have allowed to flow into them is a stream flowing down and seeking through them to reach their fellow-men".[62] So, is mystical experience an extension of evolution or a gift from above? Probably there is no contradiction for Bergson because what is "life" in its most profound sense if not the God the mystics speak of and who gives Himself to them to be given to others? It is therefore God Himself, or life, which guides humanity to a higher level through these superior spirits: "In our eyes, the ultimate end of mysticism is the establishment of a contact,

---

[60]   MR, pp. 54-55. Cf. pp. 199-200: "Would the philosophers themselves have laid down so confidently the principle, so little in keeping with everyday experience, of an equal participation of all men in a higher essence, if there had not been mystics to embrace all humanity in one simple indivisible love?".

[61]   MR, pp. 59-65, 77-79.

[62]   MR, pp. 81-82.

consequently of a partial coincidence, with the creative effort of which life is the manifestation. This effort is of God, if not God Himself. The great mystic is to be conceived as an individual being, capable of transcending the limitations imposed on the species by its material nature, thus continuing and extending the divine action".[63]

To conclude, we can say that Bergson did not seem to be interested in distinguishing between God and life. When père de Tonquédec saw a kind of pantheism in *L'évolution créatrice* he replied most clearly: "I speak of God as of the *source* from which originate, through His liberty, the 'currents' or 'élans', each of which will form a world; He remains distinct from them".[64] But this kind of discussion was probably too much like the intellectualism that he rejected. It is true that mysticism takes us close to truth (and this is why Bergson entrusted the task of elaborating this experience to philosophy), but it is not a static truth that can be contemplated intellectually, but an active, creative *movement* in which the mystic participates. We cannot know God (and here Bergson touches on an important aspect of Christianity) simply by saying that He is love, but by putting into practice this love, that is, by participating in the creation.[65] Precisely because the mystic ascends, "by turning back for fresh impetus, in the direction whence that impetus came", and this ascension comes about

---

[63] MR, p. 188. Christian mysticism differs from pagan mysticism in that it does not stop at contemplation but wishes to participate actively in the love of God for all men: in this sense Plotinus "did not get beyond this last stage, he did not reach the point where, as contemplation is engulfed in action, the human will becomes one with the divine will" (p. 188). But this intellectualistic limitation in turn should be related to the social and historical conditions of ancient times: it is only thanks to the enormous scientific and technical development of modern times that mysticism has been able to become active and go beyond the resignation of contemplation or ecstasy which is typical of backward societies. Thus the connection between Christianity, modernity and industry, the fulcrum of Western civilisation, is established (cf. pp. 193-94, 251, 267-68).

[64] Cf. C. Tresmontant, *La crise moderniste*, cit., pp. 157-58.

[65] "As a matter of fact, the mystics unanimously bear witness that God needs us, just as we need God. Why should He need us unless it be to love us? And it is to this very conclusion that the philosopher who holds to the mystical experience must come. Creation will appear to him as God undertaking to create creators, that He may have, beside Himself, beings worthy of his love... This being the case, there is nothing to prevent the philosopher from following to its logical conclusion the idea which mysticism suggests to him of a universe which is the mere visible and tangible aspect of love, and of the need of love" (MR, pp. 218-19). Bergson however admits that "creative energy", that is, God, "is to be defined as love" (p. 220).

through intuition completed by *action*, "a soul strong enough, noble enough to make this effort would not stop to ask whether the principle with which it is now in touch is the transcendent cause of all things or merely its earthly delegate".[66] In this, Bergson is closer to Loisy than Loisy would like to admit, because the originality of Bergson's metaphysics — which was not sufficiently well understood by Loisy — lies in the linking of life and action and his disregard for the need for intellectual determination; the real problem is that in the Bergsonism of *The Two Sources* Christianity acquires a unique role that Loisy is not prepared to accept.[67] Regarding the *élitist* and individualistic nature of Bergson's conception of mysticism that he has often been accused of,[68] it can be explained in part if we think that Bergson tries to speak *about God* (I mean, about a being that mankind is remote from and unprepared for, because taken up with the egoistical task of its own preservation), about a God who has loved mankind and has associated it with Himself in this love — and not about some religious or moral ideal as Loisy does. Thus, in view of the distance that separates us from God, Bergson can be pessimistic about humanity in general, for whom only static religion is *natural*;[69] on the other hand, thanks to the proximity of a moral or social ideal of progress, Loisy can be optimistic, in the sense that this ideal coincides with what is best in humanity.

5. In the twenties and thirties, Loisy, persecuted, abandoned and isolated, is drawn towards that typical, universal, work of French literature, the *Confessions* of Rousseau.[70] After the solemn, public condemnations, Loisy defends himself: he declares his innocence, he feels he is in the midst of a conspiracy and tries again and again to vindicate himself.[71] After *Choses*

---

[66] MR, pp. 180-81.

[67] As it progresses from social or natural necessities towards its vital origins, religion experiences an increase in truth: compared with the deceptions of static religion, which illude the individual in order to keep him tied to his obligations, Christian mysticism is the supreme religion, so different from other religions that we should ask whether it should still be called religion (MR, pp. 178-81).

[68] For Bergson, authentic religious experience requires exceptional qualities, a sort of "genius" like that which has produced all great artistic creations. This experience is, of course, weakly echoed in ordinary men, cf. MR, pp. 81, 182.

[69] MR, pp. 176, 179, 190, 269.

[70] It is Bremond who asserts this: "his memoires, his *confessions*, to utter the word" (SL, p. 144).

[71] On 19 March 1935 Bergson, speaking to Chevalier, says that Loisy "wrongly supposes that my book *The Two Sources* was directed against him" (J. Chevalier, *Entretiens avec Bergson*, cit., p. 221).

passées, written in 1913, in which he was still taken up with confuting the Vatican condemnations of 1907-1908, Loisy published three volumes of *Mémoires* (1930-31), a total of 1860 pages; they are memoires full of documents, letters written by him and by others, which he comments on in detail. But he only became alone, "completely alone" he confesses to Guitton,[72] when his friend Henri Bremond died on 17 August 1933; in the twenties their friendship had grown (though it was a private, almost secret friendship, for obvious political-diplomatic reasons) and Bremond had a considerable influence on Loisy's thought. At the end of a resounding speech about his friend after his death, Loisy, a precise and diffident person, wrote: "before leaving this world, I wanted to pay my respects in this short book to a man whose friendship was infinitely precious and beneficial to me... He was one of those people of whom it can be said in the words of the Gospel (*Luke* XX: 37) that theirs is 'not a God of the dead, but of the living: for all live unto him', in him and through him, for ever".[73] We should therefore try to understand the importance that the work of Bremond had in the development of Loisy's philosophy of religion and of mysticism and his influence on Loisy's confutation of Bergson, or to be more precise, the creation of a common front of the two friends against the last work of Bergson.[74]

For Loisy, Bergson's position is too philosophical, or metaphysical, for a subject, religion, that demands greater respect for historical facts;[75] the conflict can thus in part be seen as the result of their different

---

[72] Cf. CM, p. 133.

[73] TB, p. 195.

[74] This relation between Loisy and Bergson could become a group of three, with Bremond, or of four if we include E. Le Roy, Bergson's successor at the Collège de France in 1914 and friend of Bergson and Loisy. But the reflections of this Catholic Bergsonian on mysticism belong mostly to a later period (*Introduction à l'étude du problème religieux* [Paris, 1944]), apart from several discussions at the French philosophical society (like the one, already mentioned, initiated by the paper of J. Baruzi, 2 May 1925). Cf. *Bulletin de la Société française de Philosophie* (January 1926).

[75] Bergson had operated a sort of systematic suspension of history, which meant that Christology was strangely absent from his Christianity. He thought that if mysticism is only a more intense, but perfectly traditional, form of religious feeling, then philosophy did not need to concern itself with it, "for (philosophy) ignores revelation, which has a definite date, the institutions which have transmitted it, the faith that accepts it"; but if mysticism possesses an "original content, drawn straight from the very well-spring of religion", then philosophy (which confines itself to experience and inference) can concern itself with it, "to make it a powerful help-meet to philosophical research" (cf. MR, pp. 214-215).

backgrounds and professions. Paying his respects to Bremond after his death, Loisy wrote that Bergson "attempted to complete his philosophy of nature with a philosophy of the spirit", whereas they were historians who tried not to impose any extraneous constructions on reality. "The theoretical and abstract point of view that Bergson adopts is disconcerting for a spirit accustomed to see the religious and moral evolution of humanity as a vital movement, which has only to be observerd carefully in order to understand, insofar as this is possible, its general direction and the laws governing it"; "it is the transcendent, metaphysical nature of his theory that has led M. Bergson to crown it with a solution to the religious problem that we historians of religions and of religion cannot accept"; "he should not have integrated mysticism as an element or part in a purely philosophical synthesis, in the metaphysics of universal being, for the good reason that mysticism is essentially something other than metaphysics; in a certain sense it is the principle and basis of all spiritual life and cannot be included in a branch of science or in an analysis or synthesis of human concepts".[76] This mistrust of metaphysics was common to Loisy and Bremond, partly because the metaphysics they had first known, during their ecclesiastical formation, was Thomistic metaphysics (this is a hypothesis put forward by Boyer de Sainte Suzanne about the Loisy-Bergson relationship),[77] but in particular because the line of their defence, against Catholic orthodoxy, was based on this: the fundamentally superficial, inessential and constantly changing nature of the doctrinal objectivations that come from religious experience (if we like, it is the distinction between "dogmatic faith" and "mystical faith" that Bremond had made in his anonymous work in defence of Loisy).

In a letter to Loisy Bremond made a number of significant points that throw light on their relationship with Bergson: "The perception of the divine, this primary experience out of which all religions were born, is by definition *a-* or *supra-orthodox*, because it is not of a discursive nature. The discourse with which it is later interpreted and constructed will seem to us absurd or sublime. It follows that, when he puts Christianity at the top of the list, (Bergson) without a doubt moves out of the mystical order — which is also the dynamic order".[78] In the common conception of the two friends, which is a post-Christian conception (the religion of humanity, or

---

[76]　Cf. TB, pp. 177, 181, 186, 189-90 (cf. A. Harnack, WC, p. 149: "The Gospel is no theoretical doctrine or worldly wisdom". Translation modified).

[77]　BS, p. 227.

[78]　TB, p. 186.

of the spirit), Bergson inclined dangerously towards Catholic orthodoxy, or at least towards its fundamental premisses, when he legitimated — this is where metaphysics comes in — a conceptual determination of the divine. Further points separated them from Bergson: Loisy puts mysticism ("the principle and basis of all spiritual life") on a continuum with the moral and social life of humanity and thus he does not admit to a "static" phase and a "dynamic" phase of religion, except as aspects that are variable and in different degrees always present in the historical religions. For Bergson there is a breach, a leap; for Loisy there is continuity, evolution. For Bergson mysticism is a supreme, or exceptional, aspect of the evolution of life; for Loisy, as love of one's fellow-men, sacrifice in humility day after day, solidarity, it belongs to the normality of human life and permits its full realisation. Bremond did not see the question any differently: "For us there is a single source of religion and morality".[79] And it is in part thanks to Bremond and to his vast research on the mystics that Loisy consolidated his new sense of religion; Loisy writing about his book *La religion*, 1917, says: "At the beginning I did not feel the fundamental identity between the religion of humanity and the pure love of the mystics in the same way as, partly thanks to Bremond, I did later".[80] "This needs to be said without the slightest hesitation: the life of man has always been marked by renunciation aand willing sacrifice, not by transcendent revelations or high metaphysics. Certainly all his activities have contributed to a greater or lesser extent to his progress, but the deep and essential cause of his advancement has in all times been the generosity of the devotion of each individual to everyone and of everyone to each individual in organised societies".[81]

Christology is largely absent both in Bergson and in Loisy. *The Two Sources* speaks of Christ only at one point: the divinity of Christ is of little importance, given that there exists the divinity of all men; however, the great mystics "are the imitators and original continuators... of what the Christ of the Gospels was in all His glory".[82] In the philosophical-religious writings of Loisy the absence is even more obvious, if that is possible: Loisy even declared that he could "perceive a new God", that is, an ideal of humanity "better, yes, better and truer than Christ".[83] But, as Bremond

---

[79] TB, p. 187.

[80] TB, p. 148.

[81] A. Loisy, *Y a-t-il deux sources de la religion et de la morale?* (Paris, 1934) p. 202 (abbreviation RM).

[82] MR, p. 205.

[83] *Mémoires*, III (1931) p. 301.

said, Bergson puts Christianity in first place in historical evolution, and does his best to give a partially positive evaluation of Christian dogma (as the expression, communication, and also guide and point of reference, of religious experience).[84] Loisy sees it as the highest of the positive religions, the anticipation or decisive prefiguration of the future religion of humanity, but he does not believe that Christ is God or that he founded the Church, and he remains attached to Christianity as "the religion of love" without Christ. Both Loisy and Bergson speak repeatedly of God or of the Spirit, of God as love and as the mystical principle of love-devotion; they speak of the participation in divine life as the participation in this love (which, at least for Loisy, also includes the dimension of renunciation and sacrifice); but there never emerges that evangelical — and clearly anti-metaphysical — position according to which we in reality know nothing of God except what we can know in Christ. It is possible that the heritage of the Enlightenment, in the sense, for example, of an ethical or practical reduction of the Christian message like that to be found in Rousseau, had an influence on Loisy, together with the anti-metaphysical and anti-theological tendency that is hostile to a *cognitive* or speculative determination of the nature or natures of Christ. This would explain the importance given to action, to the practice of good, as the concrete and active knowledge of Christ in works,[85] all of which clearly takes us back to Harnack. Another reason for this reserve can be found in Loisy's scientific way of thinking, in a certain phenomenalism or agnosticism that privileges the manifestations (in this case the early communities of faith, the testimonies) rather than the truth or ultimate substance of a phenomenon (Christ, the object of the testimonies). Moreover, if you reject the divinity of Jesus, the relation between his person and Christianity becomes a particular case of the relation between the individual and history, which can be analysed in the usual sociological terms: "There is no question that in the past powerful enterprises determined the great reforms of religion and morality. But, taking a closer look, the great initiators of religious revolutions were all in

---

[84] Cf. H. Gouhier, *Bergson et le Christ des Evangiles* (Paris, 1961).

[85] Loisy's remarks about the "new God" just mentioned (*Mémoires*, III, p. 301), are commented on by Bremond with these words: "If I have undersood these notes rightly... the 'new God' of whom he claims to be the prophet and minister is not really new; all religions, through their dogmas and rites, have worshipped him; it is rather a new faith or a new religion that is already practised... by those, Christians and others, who dedicate themselves to good for the love of good" (SL, p. 166).

some way conditioned and prepared by the general evolution of society...
The originality of religious and moral action can be encountered
everywhere in varying degrees. The eminence of a personality may
distinguish it from others, but it does not put it on another level. However,
the bold initiative of the heroes of faith is indispensable for beneficial
revolutions to be brought about in time".[86]

6. The two friends, Loisy and Bremond, put forward a "religious
philosophy" which, like that of Bergson, placed mystical experience at the
center of their reflections; and since for them mysticism is a universal feature
of religion, they felt they were above denominational differences (Bremond
had remained in the Catholic Church) and above all particular religions.[87]
Mystical experience is described as a *sentiment*, similar to Bergson's notion
of *intuition*, because, in opposition to academic rationalism and
denominational dogmatism, they want to retain the concrete and active
nature of the experience, which comes from the totality of life and not from
an abstract theoretical elaboration.[88] Love is at the center of the discussion,
as it was in Bergson, but it does not become simply the object of faith or
sentiment, because, as in Bergson, we can comprehend it only by
participating in it. Love is the principle, in Bergson because God is love, in
Loisy because love is divine. But it is not just any kind of love: love as
principle is love as devotion, disinterested and universal love (for the whole
of humanity); it is what in the history of mysticism (the Bossuet-Fénelon
controversy) is called "pure love" and is identified with quietist
tendencies.[89] Loisy uses a variety of terms to indicate this principle (which,

---

[86] RM, pp. 195-96.
[87] Cf. TB, Ch. IV ("A religious philosophy", pp. 143-95). Expressions like "our
philosophy", p. 145, "our philosophy of religion", p. 159, are frequent in this
chapter.
[88] Cf. Loisy's review of vol. IV-V ("La Conquète mystique") of Bremond's most
important work (*Histoire littéraire du sentiment religieux en France*, Paris, 11
volumes between 1916 and 1933) in *Revue d'hist. et de litt. religieuses* (1921) pp.
564-66, and Bremond's letter in reply of 4 November 1921, cf. TB, pp. 160-61.
[89] Cf. TB, Ch. III ("The quietism of Fénelon", pp. 87-142). In contrast with Bossuet,
Fénelon and Mme Guyon upheld the doctrine of pure love: this is not to be
mistaken for moral laxism (as if mysticism, in this sense, were the reverse of
Jansenist rigorism), but rather pure love must lead to "the most total
renunciation", p. 92. Bossuet tried to show "that a degree of self-interest is
present in the virtue of charity - which excludes pure love" (pp. 103-104); on
the contrary Fénelon tried to show (in Loisy's opinion, in the more proper
tradition of Catholicism and "high mysticism": St. John of the Cross, etc.) that

it must be said, sums up the sense of his religion) and it is on the basis of this principle that he constructs a philosophy of history.

Religion, morality, society, mysticism, progress, mankind — all these concepts seem to become confused in Loisy's later writings.[90] But to have religion means to serve, through renunciation and sacrifice, society and (by progressive expansions) mankind in that most secret and ever-present nucleus that is the capacity to love without a reason, a nucleus that reveals itself slowly in time, in particular in Christianity, but that now becomes the explicit, direct theme (no longer represented metaphysically or mythically) of a universal religion.[91] This religion is a religion of *humanity*, in the sense that in it what is venerated and sought after is not humanity as it is, but humanity as it could be and substantially already is if the "pure love" of the mystics lives within it. It is a religion of the *spirit*, because, as Christianity has already proclaimed, it is not knowledge or wisdom that is spirit, but love. It is a religion of the *future*, because it presupposes the end of the great historical religions, above all Christianity, in the realisation of the principle, which those religions themselves had possessed, of love-devotion.[92]

---

the love of God and of one's fellow men is totally disinterested, p. 104. "In fact, pure love and sacrifice have always been synonyms in the language of Christianity; and they were still synonyms in the *quietism* of Fénelon and Mme Guyon" (p. 107).

[90] Cf. RM, pp. 65-66, 190, 199-202, 208-209. Numerous texts have these features: see for example *La religion*, cit., pp. 37-38, 48, and *Mémoires*, cit., III, pp. 183, 332: "human sociability and religion are in solidarity, and human progress is none other than the religious sense of humanity, an ever-growing sense, but which is destroyed if it is divested of its mystical nature".

[91] RM, pp. 129-30, 149-50, 155-56.

[92] TB, pp. 145-48, 152-56, 174-77. Cf. SL, pp. 161-62: "But what he wants to save from the successive failures of the historical religions, and of the till now highest of them all, is religion itself, i.e. that essential, living element that is realised, albeit imperfectly, in all religions". According to his draft autobiography of 1936-37, *De la croyance à la foi*, Loisy had arrived, at the time of the First World War, at a "religious faith" that attributed to Christianity a primary role in the evolution of humanity; but all the historical religions had to contribute to the formation of a "superior religion". Moreover, during the war he had seen "the impotence of all existing forms of Christianity"; "the religion of universal fraternity that in the Gospel was implicit in the mythical notion of the kingdom of God" was not realised; on the contrary, the Christian God was taken for a "national God". Thus, when in a text of 1934 he summed up the "Christian ideal" in three points - kingdom of God, peace or inner renewal and the universal community of believers - he added that these points had not been

All men, in all times, possess this love, albeit in different ways: it is so unexceptional that the normal, daily functioning of social life is assured by the willing sacrifice of so many nameless people.[93] In Loisy there is a noticeable levelling down of religious life to moral and social life, to the point that often the principle of love-devotion is referred to as solidarity, solidarism and socialism;[94] this neo-kantian and durkheimian element is also present in Bergson, in the idea of static religion, but it then gives way to the heroic and "genial" individualism of dynamic religion. It is almost as though Bergson gathers together all the social elements in a lower zone, which is that of the mere preservation of the species, and then abandons it all in favour of interiority, of liberty and of the spirit. Loisy tries to put mystical experience (as the experience of the giving of self) at the service of society; but it is always of an ideal society which gradually expands to take in the whole of humanity and which rejects a love marred by interest, and so the service of society is always also service of the spirit.[95] Also the personal relationship with God (for example during prayer) and the hope of a life beyond this world are aspects of this interest, which is not completely overcome in traditional Christianity; now Loisy insists more openly and in a decidedly post-Christian way on what had really interested him right from the beginning: the collective, public, social nature of religion.[96]

---

realised in the Catholic Church; but the "Christian ideal" or the "essence of Christianity" coincide with "the essence of human religion that can be indefinitely and increasingly realised" (CM, pp. 14, 31-32, 41-43).

[93] RM, pp. 29-31; TB, pp. 168-69. Cf. A. Loisy, *La morale humaine*, cit., pp. 298-99 ("The most difficult and the most necessary is perhaps not after all what up till now has been seen as the most glorious").

[94] RM, pp. 112-15, 117-18, 153, 204; TB, pp. 150-51. Loisy also said that "mysticism, religion and the spirit of human solidarity are probably by nature one and the same thing" (*La religion*, cit., p. 14).

[95] RM, p. 190. Cf. *Religion et humanité*, cit., p. 111: "our faith is not in human kind as such, or in our modest individualities: it is in the spirit that guides humanity and in the ideal that uplifts it". In the introduction to the second edition of *La religion* (p. 27) humanity is described as "spirit in formation, being in the course of realisation".

[96] Back in 1902, in *The Gospel and the Church* and other works, Loisy had opposed Harnack on this point: "The essence of Christianity is a *collective hope*, not an inner, personal hope" (letter to Mons. Mignot, 11 May 1902). Later, through a critical evaluation of the notion of individual salvation he arrived at a perspective "in which the religious future of man is put on a collective plane, and implies a metamorphosis of man in time and on earth" (cf. BS, pp. 65-66, 103-104, 219-21).

Thus, disregarding the questionable reasons for Bergson's approach (the fusion of *mechanics* and *mysticism* in the modern-Western formation of a complete, i.e. active, mysticism), the two friends confine themselves to rejecting the privilege granted to high Christian mysticism.[97] Bergson believes that there is a leap, a fracture between society and humanity, between a relationship of interest and the pure love of the mystics; that this leap can only be made by humanity with great difficulty, and it happens only occasionally, and when it does, always as a result of divine initiative. On the contrary, Loisy and Bremond think that pure love exists and has always existed in humanity, that it has revealed itself in history through all existing religions, going back to the most basic and primitive ones; and after the disappearance of the dogmatic or mythological forms, it is this love that has for us the features of the Godhead. The question of individual salvation is a metaphysical question we cannot speak about,[98] but the effort and sacrifice that are our contribution to the evolution of humanity are certainly retained in that kingdom of justice and peace that humanity awaits, and of which the mythical image of the Kingdom of God was only a prefiguration.[99]

We can thus see the evolution of Loisy's philosophy of religion: from a radical affirmation of divine transcendence, as he moves from "dogmatic faith" to "mystical faith" he empties that transcendence and divinifies humanity as "spirit". This change occurs, in a clearly comprehensible way, when (and here he is diametrically opposed to Bergson) mystical experience is declared to have no cognitive valency and no doctrinal content, such that it is fundamentally the same in all religions; indeed Bergson is accused of not having gone further than the *static* dimension because he did not see beyond Christianity as the form of expression of the love of the mystics.[100] It is clear what Loisy and Bremond mean: love is the fiery

---

[97] RM, pp. IV-VI; TB, pp. 170-71, 183.

[98] TB, pp. 110-112. The success of the "doctrine of predestination" of Jansenism comes, according to Loisy, from a certain need for security and from the difficulty in raising oneself to a purely spiritual concept of religion, like that of the "pure love" of the mystics.

[99] Cf. A. Loisy, *Guerre et religion* (Paris, 1915) pp. 78-80; *Mors et Vita* (Paris, 1916) pp. 84-85; *La paix des Nations et la religion de l'avenir* (Paris, 1919) pp. 18-30. Already in 1917 he wrote to Boyer: "The religion of the future will be increasingly realised outside Christianity" (letter of 13 November 1917, BS, p.168).

[100] RM, p. 61; TB, pp. 118-19, 135-36, 159-60.

substance which, when it cools down, takes on many forms, it inspires doctrines, life-systems and visions of the world, but it should never be confused with any of these, even the best or the most elevated. In this way, God as love that transcends man becomes more lofty and more remote, the horizon vanishes and what comes to the fore are the "modern" reasonings of morality and science, the need (a need of the times) to express that fiery substance in words that are comprehensible to today's (or of course we should say yesterday's) humanity. Loisy's concern is to demonstrate the universal accessibility of the mystical "way" and this is why he is careful to leave aside the more overtly philosophical or metaphysical features; but although Bergson declares that the mystical way is difficult or rare, for him this rarity is not a question of obstacles in the intellectual sphere; what he means is that it is a risky or dangerous experience that could break us and that requires particular faculties of the emotions or sentiment.[101]

Like Bergson, Loisy aimed at a kind of evolutionary interpretation of religion, in the sense that its truth, its ultimate form, emerges progressively through history. The "spirit", or love-devotion, has always been present in humanity but the dogmatic or metaphysical representations of traditional religion have, as it were, falsified it for too long by showing it to the world as transcendent and thus preventing it from appearing in its full light. So, the essence-manifestation, kernel-husk distinction that Harnack used so extensively in his philosophy of history (but which was also more generally present in liberal Protestantism in the second half of the nineteenth century), is still to be found in the later works of Loisy, because it is history that gradually reveals the (human) essence of religion.

To conclude this study, there is one more important, and difficult, theme to look into: that of suffering. After his condemnation Loisy still felt himself to be Catholic on account of an intense bond with those who suffered the persecution of the Church.[102] One of the limits of Modernism is that it often fails to see poverty, isolation and emargination as fundamental or general problems of humanity but it concerns itself predominantly with those who have been condemned by the Church, and consequently its main aim is the accurate reconstruction of its own history, its own defence and that of its friends and sympathisers. Modernism is a milieu, an international milieu, but it is made up of a relatively small

---

[101] RM, pp. 39-40; MR, pp. 181-82, 188-89.
[102] "He is no longer Catholic except for the immense, still fraternal compassion that the suffering of persecuted Catholics inspires in him" (SL, p. 158).

number of people who, understandably, feel united by a particular type of misfortune (of having been excluded or emarginated from a life they had loved, the life of the Catholic Church) and who are often not able to go beyond the particularity of their situation and see it as part of the universal human situation, of the numerous forms of isolation or emargination that have nothing to do with the Catholic Church. Loisy was profoundly aware of the two sides of the problem: he suffered on account of the narrowness of this milieu which had been fragmented and dispersed by the excommunications (or even only by the suspicions and rumours) but he also saw the wider implications, which he tried to solve with his religion of humanity. This inherited from Christianity the idea that the giving of self, or of one's life, (i.e. renunciation and sacrifice) are the purest forms of the love of one's fellow-men, and it put this into practice in a solidaristic and socialistic sense, as if the sight of universal suffering were too devastating to think of God in the usual traditional terms, and any desire to do so were a kind of inadmissible luxury, a crime of lèse-humanity. This is precisely what Loisy saw in Bergson's interpretation of mysticism: not a bond with suffering humanity, but isolation in an exceptional, privileged condition, in which communion with God can only be an illusion.[103] The neglect of Christology by both Loisy and Bergson meant that they both lost sight of the idea of a God who suffers, of a God who lowers Himself to the condition of servant; thus, on one side of the discussion, human suffering came to be considered the real problem, which the advancement of humanity in love and in sacrifice could alleviate, but which was nothing to do with a transcendent God; on the other side, the exceptionality of mystical experience meant it was seen as a super-human undertaking, comparable to that of great artists, and essentially having no connection with the purely human cycle of the material preservation of life.

Moreover, the absence of a Church, of a community to refer to, is not simply an external fact that adds to the picture, but it has a profound influence on the very content of the religion. Early on Loisy had felt that this content could be determined historically or theologically and the communities to refer to were clearly the associations of scholars, the universities and the Catholic Church. But at this point there were no longer any links with the Church (or its theology) and Loisy thought he could replace it with free associations that in some way represented his point of view: the ministers of the new religion would not concern themselves with religious practices, but with moral education and they would organise

---

[103] RM, pp. 169-70, 187.

themselves into "corporations of high mystics" for the uplifting of humanity.[104] Also the growth of international institutions (the Society of Nations) could be the expression of the unification of the world in love and mutual respect, i.e. of the new religion of humanity.[105] But these vague ideas did not give mysticism a community dimension, rather they contributed to its maintaining its liberal-individualistic tendencies, which ended up by negating all content of the religion. Like any man who has been hurt, hurt too much to forget and begin again, even in his later years Loisy insisted on the *secret* nature of the mystical relationship: "the dialogue with God can come under the control of no-one... This ecstasy, this love, this pure sense of the divine, beyond all formulas, is pure love... The official Church, the ecclesiastical hierarchy, would not be able to reach it with its ordinances, it is beyond its control". In fact, Loisy explained, as Bremond had before him, that the indeterminateness of content and doctrine of mystical experience is neither intended nor contrived because during this experience the intellectual, or strictly cognitive, faculties are momentarily suspended.[106] Mysticism is of interest to Loisy and Bremond on account of the interiority (freedom) of the religious relationship, of the linguistic and conceptual renewal that, compared with scholastic theology, it favours, or presupposes; but also, inevitably, because it is invisible, uncontrollable and undefinable. In this sense, the psychology of escape (the fear of being controlled, the need to defend himself) was not resolved even after Loisy was no longer in the Catholic Church, and this obstructs any realisation, any social and historical manifestation, of the new religion of humanity.

---

[104] TB, p. 147.
[105] RM, pp. 208-209. Cf. *La paix des Nations et la religion de l'avenir*, cit.
[106] TB, pp. 118-19, 135-36.

Index

South Florida Studies in the History of Judaism

240084	Judaic Law from Jesus to the Mishnah	Neusner
240085	Writing with Scripture: Second Printing	Neusner/Green
240086	Foundations of Judaism: Second Printing	Neusner
240087	Judaism and Zoroastrianism at the Dusk of Late Antiquity	Neusner
240088	Judaism States Its Theology	Neusner
240089	The Judaism behind the Texts I.A	Neusner
240090	The Judaism behind the Texts I.B	Neusner
240091	Stranger at Home	Neusner
240092	Pseudo-Rabad: Commentary to Sifre Deuteronomy	Basser
240093	FromText to Historical Context in Rabbinic Judaism	Neusner
240094	Formative Judaism	Neusner
240095	Purity in Rabbinic Judaism	Neusner
240096	Was Jesus of Nazareth the Messiah?	McMichael
240097	The Judaism behind the Texts I.C	Neusner
240098	The Judaism behind the Texts II	Neusner
240099	The Judaism behind the Texts III	Neusner
240100	The Judaism behind the Texts IV	Neusner
240101	The Judaism behind the Texts V	Neusner
240102	The Judaism the Rabbis Take for Granted	Neusner
240103	From Text to Historical Context in Rabbinic Judaism V. II	Neusner
240104	From Text to Historical Context in Rabbinic Judaism V. III	Neusner
240105	Samuel, Saul, and Jesus: Three Early Palestinian Jewish Christian Gospel Haggadoth	Aus
240106	What is Midrash? And a Midrash Reader	Neusner
240107	Rabbinic Judaism: Disputes and Debates	Neusner
240108	Why There Never Was a "Talmud of Caesarea"	Neusner
240109	Judaism after the Death of "The Death of God"	Neusner
240110	Approaches to Ancient Judaism	Neusner
240111	Ecology of Religion	Neusner
240112	The Judaic Law of Baptism	Neusner
240113	The Documentary Foundation of Rabbinic Culture	Neusner
240114	Understanding Seeking Faith, Volume Four	Neusner
240115	Paul and Judaism: An Anthropological Approach	Laato
240116	Approaches to Ancient Judaism, New Series, Volume Eight	Neusner
240117	The Talmud of the Land of Israel, A Complete Outline of the Second, Third, and Fourth Divisions, II. A	Neusner
240118	The Talmud of the Land of Israel, A Complete Outline of the Second, Third, and Fourth Divisions, II. B	Neusner

South Florida Academic Commentary Series

The Talmud of Babylonia, An Academic Commentary

243001	Bavli, Volume XI, Tractate Moed Qatan	Neusner
243002	Bavli, Volume XXXIV, Tractate Keritot	Neusner
243003	Bavli, Volume XVII, Tractate Sotah	Neusner
243004	Bavli, Volume XXIV, Tractate Makkot	Neusner
243005	Bavli, Volume XXXII, Tractate Arakhin	Neusner

| 243043 | Bavli, Volume XIII, Tractate Yebamot, A. Chapters One through Eight | Neusner |
| 243044 | Bavli, XIII, Tractate Yebamot, B. Chapters Nine through Seventeen | Neusner |

South Florida-Rochester-Saint Louis Studies on Religion and the Social Order

245001	Faith and Context, Volume 1	Ong
245002	Faith and Context, Volume 2	Ong
245003	Judaism and Civil Religion	Breslauer
245004	The Sociology of Andrew M. Greeley	Greeley
245005	Faith and Context, Volume 3	Ong
245006	The Christ of Michelangelo	Dixon
245007	From Hermeneutics to Ethical Consensus Among Cultures	Bori
245008	Mordecai Kaplan's Thought in a Postmodern Age	Breslauer
245009	No Longer Aliens, No Longer Strangers	Eckardt
245010	Between Tradition and Culture	Ellenson
245011	Religion and the Social Order	Neusner
245012	Christianity and the Stranger	Nichols
245013	The Polish Challenge	Czosnyka

South Florida International Studies in Formative Christianity and Judaism

242501	The Earliest Christian Mission to 'All Nations'	La Grand
242502	Judaic Approaches to the Gospels	Chilton
252403	The "Essence of Christianity"	Rosa